T H E

TOUGH

KID

B O O K

Practical Classroom Management Strategies

Ginger Rhode, Ph.D.   William R. Jenson, Ph.D.   H. Kenton Reavis, Ed.D.

Tough Kid illustrations by Tom Oling
Cover design by Vicki Londerville
Text layout and design by Sherri Rowe
Edited by Jami Leutheuser

ISBN #0-944584-55-1

Published and Distributed by

SOPRIS WEST, INC.

1140 Boston Avenue • Longmont, CO 80501 • (303) 651-2829

Tough Kid Authors

Ginger Rhode, Ph.D.

Dr. Rhode is a district administrator of programs for students with moderate to severe disabilities and Youth-in-Custody students in a Utah school district of 79,000. Previous assignments have included elementary school principal, junior high school vice principal, and teacher in elementary and secondary classrooms for severe behavior disordered/emotionally disturbed students. Dr. Rhode is an adjunct faculty member at both Utah State University and the University of Utah, and has published numerous journal articles, book chapters, and professional papers. Her main areas of interest and expertise include classroom and school-wide management, social skills training, generalization and maintenance of behavior, and legal issues affecting students with disabilities.

William R. Jenson, Ph.D.

Dr. Jenson graduated from Utah State University in 1976 with a degree in Applied Behavior Analysis/School Psychology. He completed a clinical internship at Las Vegas Mental Health Center and later directed their Adolescent Residential Center. He then assumed the directorship of the Children's Behavior Therapy Unit (CBTU) for Salt Lake Mental Health. This center is a day school for autistic and behaviorally disordered students. After directing CBTU for eight years, Dr. Jenson joined the School Psychology Program in the Educational Psychology Department at the University of Utah. Dr. Jenson is currently  professor and chair of the Department of Educational Psychology. His research interests include the management of severe students, practical classroom behavior management, behavioral assessment, academic interventions, and parent training. Dr. Jenson has published several books, classroom products, and numerous research papers. For the past fifteen years, he has been an active inservice presenter and consultant for many school districts, mental health centers, and parent organizations.

H. Kenton Reavis, Ed.D.

Dr. Reavis is a specialist for behavior disorders and discipline and is the Comprehensive System of Personnel Development coordinator in the Services for At Risk Section of the Utah State Office of Education. Dr. Reavis has over twenty-five years of educational experience in the field as a classroom teacher, university professor, and administrator. His research, writing, and presentations focus on student management, discipline, school climate, noncompliance, school assistance teams, and prereferral strategies for teachers, administrators, resource personnel, and parents.

Table of Contents

Chapter 4: Advanced Systems for Tough Kids 89

What This Book Will Do For You

A major reason teachers leave teaching is because of the problems they encounter with difficult students and loss of control in their classrooms. Aggression, arguing, tantrums, and poor academic progress, coupled with difficult interactions with parents make teachers feel like failures. These problems are compounded by excessive time demands placed on them by their difficult students. This time drain leaves many teachers with a sense of powerlessness and little time to teach. Problematic students with severe classroom behaviors, a loss of control, and not enough time to instruct have a dramatic impact on teachers' job self-esteem and satisfaction.

This book will help teachers manage the "Tough Kid." Tough Kids are students that are generally not covered in most college courses in education. It is estimated that approximately two to five percent of all students meet our definition of a Tough Kid. This is enough to ensure that at least one or two tough students will be in each classroom every year. Often the number is greater.

This book is intended for use by both regular education and special education teachers who want effective and positively focused classrooms. The purpose of this book is to give teachers **practical** techniques that can be implemented without great cost in materials, time, or money. However, nothing is free. The time required to implement the suggested techniques should be viewed by teachers as a wise investment. While some initial teacher time and planning are needed, the techniques will provide educational dividends in managing difficult students in the long run that clearly outweigh the initial investments.

To achieve these goals, this book is divided into four basic chapters. The first is a getting started chapter, **What Does a Tough Kid Look Like?**, which helps teachers understand why behavior problems occur and how to practically define the Tough Kid. This chapter also covers the realistic assessment of difficult students and proactive methods of setting up a classroom. The second chapter, **Unique Positive Procedures**, focuses on interventions that can be used to reward students for coming to school, following classroom procedures,

"I quit!"

and performing academically. It is critically important that positive procedures are used with Tough Kids before reductive procedures (procedures that stop behaviors) because:

- the majority of these Tough Kids have a long history of punishment to which they have grown immune,

- they have a high risk for school dropout (estimated to be 65%) and will not stay in nonpositive environments, and

- in the long run, permanent behavior changes are maintained only by basic positive procedures.

If punishment-oriented reductive techniques are the

"Pointer Box"

most frequently used techniques in a classroom, then these students will simply stop coming to school.

This book, however, does not espouse a totally reward-based approach. The third chapter of the book, **Practical Reductive Techniques for the Classroom**, reviews realistic techniques that can be used by teachers to stop problem behaviors. The authors recognize that some reductive techniques are needed to quickly manage such behaviors as aggression, noncompliance, arguing, and tantrums. Behavior reducing techniques are important for teachers in stopping the "pain control" that is frequently used by Tough Kids. If these techniques are not examined, they are generally improperly or excessively used by untrained classroom staff.

The last book chapter is entitled **Advanced Systems for Tough Kids** because these techniques are more complex in nature. Techniques covered as advanced procedures include social skills training materials, instructional techniques, programs to improve on-task behavior, parent training information, and more. The more advanced techniques are viewed as finishing procedures

that allow a teacher to develop beyond the basic procedures presented in the first three sections of the book.

In addition to the chapter divisions of the book, there are a series of **Boxes**, **Figures**, **Pointer Boxes**, and **How To Boxes** in each chapter. No single book can give teachers all the techniques and information they need. The **Pointer Boxes** are designed to **point** teachers to additional resources if they are interested in pursuing a topic in more detail or want specific classroom materials (e.g., references for more in depth coverage of a technique, commercially available materials, etc.). Similar to the **Pointer Boxes** are the **How To Boxes**. These boxes are designed to give teachers step-by-step instructions on designing and implementing a particular technique (e.g., how to design a school-home note, or implementing a program such as the "Sure I Will" program).

A note of caution. Teachers should recognize that they cannot immediately implement all the techniques presented in this book. Such a task would be overwhelming. An effective strategy for teachers is to select those techniques that best fit their classrooms. However, it is very important for teachers not to skip or halfheartedly implement the suggested positive classroom techniques. A positive classroom is the foundation for all other techniques recommended in this book.

Basic classroom interventions, "pointers" to additional material, and "how to" instructions are all important. But what is fundamental is a common understanding and definition of a "Tough Kid." If we do not have a common definition, it is difficult to come to a consensus on how to manage and educate these students.

Chapter 1

What Does a Tough Kid Look Like?

Most of us believe we can recognize tough or difficult students. To have one in your classroom is to recognize one. They can make our teaching lives miserable and single-handedly disrupt a classroom. They hurt others. They are disruptive. They do not learn easily. They are not well-liked.

These students come with a plethora of labels such as behavior disordered, seriously emotionally disturbed, at risk, conduct disordered, oppositional disordered, antisocial, and attention deficit disordered, to name a few. While the labels are different, these students have common traits and behaviors that are easy for us to identify.

> "To have one in your classroom is to recognize one."

Excesses

There is a definition which incorporates these characteristics and also allows us to design educational procedures to help Tough Kids. First, Tough Kids stand out and are referred for special services because of particular excessive types of behavior. They argue with teachers. They are commonly defiant when given a request by adults or peers. If pressed, these students commonly increase the ante and become aggressive or tantrum.

"King Pin"

The central characteristic of Tough Kids is frequency or **degree**. They frequently will not follow adult requests. Or, they habitually break classroom or school rules. Average students are also to some degree noncompliant, argue, tantrum, and occasionally fight. But the key to this description is the word "degree." Tough Kids have a high degree or frequency of these **behavioral excesses** (noncompliance, arguing, tantrum throwing, rule breaking, etc.). They show too much of these behaviors.

Noncompliance and Coercion

A "king-pin" is something that is central or holds something together. Tough Kids have a king-pin behavior that is central to their behavioral excesses. This king-pin or axle around which other behavioral excesses revolve is **non-**

compliance. Noncompliance is simply defined as not following a direction within a reasonable amount of time. Most of the arguing, tantrums, fighting, or rule breaking is secondary to avoiding requests or required tasks. When you ask a Tough Kid to do a simple task (e.g., the assigned work) the student may argue or tantrum to get you to rescind or withdraw the request. Once the teacher withdraws or reduces the request, then the arguing and tantrum throwing is rewarded. This process has been called "pain control" or "coercion" because painful behavior (i.e., arguing, whining, excuse-making, delays, tantrums, aggression, and property destruction) are used to force a request to be withdrawn by the teacher (Patterson, 1982). This coercive process between a student and teacher is outlined in How To Box 1-1, and is fundamental to understanding Tough Kids' problems.

When a student's compliance to an adult's request falls below **40%**, then noncompliance is excessive enough to disable a student. At this point the student stands out in the teacher's mind as difficult and tough. Most students comply to about 80% of a teacher's requests. Tough Kids comply to 40% or less of a teacher's requests. A simple way to test compliance rates is to keep track of a series of everyday commands given to students in the classroom. If a teacher gives an average of ten commands and the student responds to four or less of these commands, then the student meets our definition of tough. This simple approach in assessing compliance is covered in more detail later in this chapter.

Behavioral Deficits

There is an insidious by-product to being coercive. The student typically does not learn or develop like other students in the classroom. If the student uses the pain control behaviors of arguing, aggression, excuse-making, and throw-

ing a tantrum to avoid compliance, then basic skill development in other areas is arrested. Teachers ask students to do academic assignments to develop **basic academic skills**. If coercion is used with the teacher, then the child develops an academic deficit. Similarly, students interact in give-and-take social exchanges. If a student uses coercive behaviors to always get his/her way with peers, then **social skills** do not develop. If a student expects each demand to be immediately met or he/she engages in coercive behaviors, then the student develops a

"A Game of One-on-One"

deficit in learning to delay gratification and abide by rules. In other words, the Tough Kid develops a deficit in **self-management skills or rule following behavior**.

It is easy to identify the behavioral excesses in students. These are the behaviors that commonly get Tough Kids referred for special services. However, most of the real work comes in identifying and remediating the behavioral deficits found in these students. The longer a student successfully engages in coercive pain control to avoid requests, then the more profound the behavioral deficits. Even if coercion is eventually stopped, few students can be successful with significant deficits in basic academics, social skills, and self-management.

How To Box 1-1

Coercive Pain Control
(Or, How to Make It Worse)

Problems in compliance only occur after a request is made and the student is expected to obey. Read the steps below and follow along with the requests made in Figure 1-1. Imagine a teacher trying to get a student to do his/her in-seat mathematics assignment.

Step 1: The teachers asks, "Bubba, **wouldn't you like to** hurry and get this assignment finished?" Bubba **ignores** the question-request. If you think about it, this is not too smart of a question.

Step 2: The teacher then tries to cajole and humor Bubba into working with, "**Come on please**, I will help you with the first problem." Bubba now **delays** and says "Wait just a minute, I'll finish it when I'm done drawing my picture."

Step 3: After several minutes of doing nothing but doodling, the teacher now **yells**, "**Now you had better** do it! I'm not going to ask again." Bubba now **argues**, "You always pick on me, you have never liked me." Or, **makes an excuse**, "Can't you see I am having a tough day, and you still push me?"

Step 4: Still noncompliance, and the teacher is upset and ready to do something. She overdoes it and yells, "**Now you have had it!** Get to the principal's office. If you are not going to work, you can't be in my class." Bubba explodes. He becomes **aggressive and tantrums**.

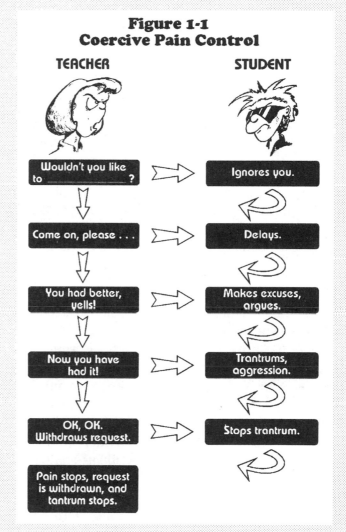

Figure 1-1
Coercive Pain Control

TEACHER STUDENT

Wouldn't you like to _____? → Ignores you.

Come on, please . . . → Delays.

You had better, yells! → Makes excuses, argues.

Now you have had it! → Trantrums, aggression.

OK, OK. Withdraws request. → Stops trantrum.

Pain stops, request is withdrawn, and tantrum stops.

Step 5: The teacher is so upset, she feels it is not worth pushing Bubba. She thinks "He is too touchy–I don't care if he doesn't learn." The teacher withdraws her request by simply walking away and doing nothing. When this happens:

• Bubba is reinforced for all his disruptive behavior (ignoring, delaying, arguing, and throwing a tantrum).

• Bubba stops throwing his tantrum, and the teacher is reinforced for withdrawing her request.

Academic Deficits

One of the best predictors of long term adjustment for Tough Kids is basic academic skills, particularly reading (as reviewed by Gelfand, Jenson, & Drew, 1988). If students have not learned to read, they are not likely to be successfully employed in our technology-oriented society. Reading is a critical skill. If they cannot find work because they have difficulty reading, then many of these students fall back on old excessive behavioral strategies and are arrested as adolescents and adults for assault or theft. Approximately 41% of all behaviorally disordered students are arrested within two years of separation from school (U.S. Office of Education, 1991). The basic academic skills of reading, mathematics, writing, and spelling are essential, and coercion cannot be allowed to stop their development. A section in the **Advanced Systems for Tough Kids** chapter of this book presents a number of strategies and curricula that can be successfully used with these students. However, academic deficits are common in Tough Kids.

Parallel behaviors that are critical in the development of academic skills are basic **on-task behavior** and **academic learning** time (Hofmeister & Lubke, 1988). Academic learning time will be covered in more detail in the assessment section of this chapter. However, many coercive Tough Kids are frequently off-task. These students simply do not pay attention to the teacher during lectures nor to their written work. They frequently talk to other students, daydream, doodle, make noises, or play with objects. The average student in a classroom is on-task approximately 85% of the time. During this time, they actively attend to the teacher and their assigned work. The Tough Kid's average on-task behavior is only about 60% or less of teacher-directed instruction or in-seat work activities. This 20% or more on-task difference between Tough Kids and their peers has a dramatic impact on academic skill development. When Tough Kids remain off-task, they fall

"Of course I can read."

further and further behind other students. Their on-task rate must be increased to at least an 85% level. Several techniques and packages for improving on-task behaviors are also given in the **Advanced Systems for Tough Kids** chapter.

Social Skills

Primary social skills are simply defined as the basic skills needed to successfully interact with adults and peers. These skills include foundation skills such as how to start a conversation, grooming, entering games, cooperation, and giving appropriate positive feedback to others. Intermediate to advanced socials skills build on the foundation skills and include the more complicated skills of accepting negative feedback, learning how to say "No," assertiveness, resisting peer pressure, resisting teasing, managing anger, and other skills. We want all students to have and use social skills. However, if they have not developed these skills naturally over time, then they must be taught them just like any other basic skill.

Tough Kids who use coercive pain control to manage peers generally have not developed the basic foundation and intermediate social skills they need. These students are often described as socially immature, pushy, noncooperative, bullies, or students who must always be in control.

Frequently, these Tough Kids go through a series of friendships that do not last. This rapid turnover in friends occurs because other students do not like their dominating interactions. If pain control coercion retards social skills development, then Tough Kids often choose younger friends or may interact with other students who have similar behavior problems. Tough Kids pick these types of friends because they are easily dominated, and their social skills are on a par with them.

Tough Kids' social skills generally do not evolve appropriately. Even if the behavioral excesses and coercion are stopped, these students are still deficit in their basic social skills. If they are not taught appropriate replacement social skills, they will revert back to their old coercive strategies when interacting with their peers. These skills must be taught, practiced, and then tried in natural peer interactions to be successful. Several research-validated social skills programs are listed in the **Advanced Systems for Tough Kids** chapter along with guidelines for teaching these skills. In addition, assessment of these skills is covered later in this chapter.

Rule Following and Self-Management

The final characteristic of Tough Kids is a lack of rule following and self-management skills. Most teachers and parents would like Tough Kids to "internalize" a set of values and naturally behave like other students. A common complaint by teachers is "Why can't they behave like other students?" The problem is that these student do not internalize commonly accepted values. They simply want immediate gratification. Guilt questions that involve values such as "What would your parents think?" or "Imagine how that makes him feel?" or "Can't you see how that hurts others?" simply do not work. We can wait forever for the magical inculcation of appropriate values from family,

teachers, peers, and community, but it simply will not happen.

The concept of the internalization of values may be a mistake in the education of Tough Kids. It is too easy to blame these students or their families for this failure of values internalization, which only makes things worse. A more functional concept is to recognize that coercive pain control leads to demands for immediate gratification. This is why Tough Kids are frequently described as impulsive, demanding, uncooperative, and attention-getting. When this coercive process takes place, the basic skills of learning to wait for gratification and abiding by rules are stunted. It may be less a problem of the internalization of values and more a problem of not learning basic self-management skills.

Self-management skills are skills that are learned in order to put off immediate gratification for a long-term benefit. In other words, students learn to practically manage their immediate wants for a later benefit. Rules (from society, schools, classrooms, families) are often shorthand guides for self-managing behavior. If a rule is broken, there is a consequence. When these guidelines or rules become habits, we often refer to them as internalized. That is, the student is rule-governed. The basic steps for the development of self-management or rule-governed behavior are listed below (Skinner, 1953).

- Step 1: Learning to comply to requests

- Step 2: Learning self-control

- Step 3: Learning problem solving skills

With Tough Kids, consistency and immediate consequences for either following or breaking rules is essential. If teachers are consistent in applying consequences to rules, then the student will learn consistency as a habit. If teachers are inconsistent, then the student will learn inconsistency as a habit and will continue with coercion. Advanced self-management skills are taught in some social skills training programs and some self-management packages (Young, West, Smith, & Morgan, 1991). These packages are reviewed in the **Advanced Systems for Tough Kids** chapter.

Our overall definition of a Tough Kid is a student who has behavioral excesses and deficits.

The excesses that make the student stand out include noncompliance, arguing, excuse-making, throwing tantrums and aggression. The equally important but often overlooked deficits include deficiencies in basic academic and social skills, and rule following and self-management skills (see Box 1-1).

Not all students exactly fit this model definition of a Tough Kid. Some Tough Kids may be socially skilled or have academic ability; however, these are exceptions to the general rule. Most Tough Kids will have one or more of these characteristics. Thus, it becomes important to teach practical assessment of these excesses and deficits.

Box 1-1

Practical Definition of a Tough Kid

Behavior Excesses: *Too much of a behavior.*

- Noncompliance

    - Does not do what is requested
    - Breaks rules
    - Argues
    - Makes excuses
    - Delays
    - Does the opposite of what is asked

- Aggression

    - Tantrums
    - Fights
    - Destroys property
    - Vandalizes
    - Sets fires
    - Teases
    - Verbally abuses
    - Is revengeful
    - Is cruel to others

Behavioral Deficits: *Inability to Adequately Perform a Behavior.*

- Self-Management Skills

    - Cannot delay rewards
    - Acts before thinking—impulsive
    - Shows little remorse or guilt
    - Will not follow rules
    - Cannot foresee consequences

- Social Skills

    - Has few friends
    - Goes through friends fast
    - Noncooperative—bossy
    - Does not know how to reward others
    - Lacks affection
    - Has few problem-solving skills
    - Constantly seeks attention

- Academic Skills

    - Generally behind in academics, particularly reading
    - Off-task
    - Fails to finish work
    - Truant or frequently tardy
    - Forgets acquired information easily

Practical Assessment of Tough Kids

A teacher might ask, "Why is assessment necessary for Tough Kids?" To have one in your class is to know one. However, assessment becomes important for the following reasons:

1. To accurately identify a student, particularly if requests or referrals for additional help are made.

2. To determine the exact problem behavior(s) that will require some type of program.

3. To use a standard measurement approach to evaluation to determine whether progress is made after a program is started.

Assessment is merely structured information gathering. The information gathered is generally worthless unless it can be used to design an intervention to help the student. However, there can be problems even with assessment techniques that are designed for program interventions. All assessment procedures are imperfect and have error associated with them. There are no perfect assessment methods. To reduce error and improve decisions, it is important to use **multiple assessment measures** and assessment techniques that are **standardized**.

Multiple measures simply means that two or more assessment methods or raters (assessors) are used to measure the problem behavior in question. If multiple/valid measures are used, then the errors in each tend to cancel each other out, and a much more accurate result is obtained. It is good practice to use a variety of assessment measures such as behavior checklists, social skills checklists, curriculum probes, and in-class observations for difficult students. It is also wise to use more than one rater. For example, two teachers are better than one. Or, parents can be used, or even the students themselves.

Standardization usually means that the measure has good reliability and validity. Reliability is a direct measure of consistency. If the measure is given twice we should get similar results (test-retest reliability). Similarly, if the measure is used by two different people on the same student, then the result should be similar (inter-rater reliability). Reliability measures how consistent an assessment result will be either across time or across raters.

Validity is an indicator of a measure/test's reality. A valid assessment method truly measures what it purports to measure. If a behavioral checklist purports to identify attention deficit hyperactivity disordered (ADHD) students, but systematically omits several ADHD students, then it has poor validity. Teachers should be consumer-conscious and ask about the reliability and validity of assessment measures they are asked to give. Reliability of .80 or greater is generally considered good for most assessment methods. Good assessment measures also describe validity studies in their instruction manuals. Ask to see them.

Standardization also allows the determination of whether a student is truly disabled and different from his/her average peers. This is important because what one teacher thinks is exceptional or aberrant may seem very average to another. Most good assessment measures are based on standardization groups of hundreds of students. When the measures were first developed, average scores (means) for typical, nondisabled students were established. These scores were determined for classroom behaviors, social skills, and academic abilities, and can be especially useful when identifying and working with Tough Kids. For example, we know the scores are distributed on a normal bell-shaped curve (see Figure 1-2) with the mean score located

Figure 1-2
Normal Curve With Figures of Tough Kids

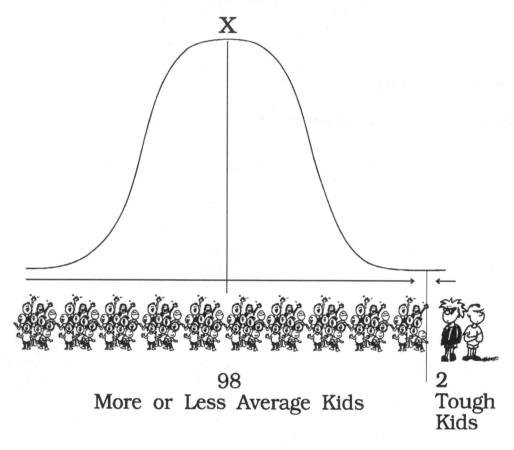

98
More or Less Average Kids

2
Tough
Kids

right in the middle of the curve (where the "X" is on the curve).

A standard deviation is a measure of variability and can help define deviant or abnormal scores. A score two standard deviations up from the mean score is a very different score and helps define Tough Kids. It signifies that only two percent of students in the original standardization group had scores this high and different. Picture in your mind a group of 100 students lined up against a wall (see Figure 1-2). Each student represents an increasingly different score from the first student in line. Only the last two students in the line of 100 students would have scores different enough to be two standard deviations above the mean score (or above the 98th percentile).

The two standard deviation method gives us an objective technique to determine if a student is truly tough. If several teachers or aides (multiple measure raters) fill out behavior checklists on a student, and his/her scores fall two standard deviations from the mean, then he/she meets our definition of tough.

Two common ways for behavior checklists and other tests to express this standard deviation difference are **T** and **Z standard** scores. The mean T score is always 50, with a two standard deviation which is always 70 or higher. A mean Z score is always zero (0), with a two standard deviation of two. For example, an Aggression score of T-70 or above on the ***Child Behavior Checklist*** (Achenbach & Edelbrock, 1983) would put a student two standard deviations from the mean, or above the 98th percentile–a truly tough student.

Checklists

Basic standardized checklists can be very useful for teachers in identifying Tough Kids and their problem behavior. Checklists are generally easy to use, economical, have good reliability and validity, and are standardized. **Problem behavior checklists** frequently give lists of behaviors with definitions, and teachers are asked to rate each behavior along a dimension (i.e, "very true," "sometimes true," or "not true"). See the example below from the **Child Behavior Checklist**.

	very true	sometimes true	not true
3. Argues a lot	2	1	0

The checklists do not require actual observation of the student, but a teacher is asked to recall the behavior and make a judgment as to its severity. Good behavior checklists are standardized and allow the two standard deviation comparisons described above. In addition, some behavior checklists come with a variety of parallel forms that allow several raters to fill out the checklists (multiple measures). For example, the *Child Behavior Checklist* has parallel forms for the teacher, parent, and even the student. A source list of standardized checklists is supplied in Pointer Box 1-1.

Similar to problem behavior checklists are **social skills checklists**. They differ from problem behavior checklists in that they do not identify problem behaviors, but rather, they identify social skills deficits. These checklist are rated on similar dimensions (see the following example from the *Social Skills Rating System*, Gresham & Elliot, 1990) and allow standard deviation comparisons to see if a problem genuinely exists.

5. Politely refuses unreasonable requests from others–rate as					
HOW OFTEN			HOW IMPORTANT		
never	some-times	very often	not impor-tant	impor-tant	critical
1	2	3	1	2	3

Some social skills checklists also have multiple parallel forms for the teacher, parent, and student. Some good social skills checklists are listed in Pointer Box 1-2.

Both behavior and social skills checklists help teachers pinpoint behavioral excesses and deficits in Tough Kids. They can even indicate the severity of a problem if the standard deviation method of comparison is used. However, they do not give a direct practical measure of non-compliance, which we have already identified as the "king pin" behavior problem for Tough Kids. To get this compliance measure, direct teacher probes are most useful.

Pointer Box 1-1

Sources for Problem Behavior Checklists

Behavior Evaluation Scale
S. McCarney, J. Leigh, & J. Cornbleet
Associated Management Systems
P.O. Box 510
Vernon, AL 35592-0510

Behavior Rating Profile (Teacher Form)
L. Brown & D. Hammill
Pro-Ed Publishing Co.
5341 Industrial Oakes Boulevard
Austin, TX 78735

Child Behavior Checklist (Teacher, Parent, Youth Report Form)
T. M. Achenbach
University Associates in Psychiatry
1 South Prospect Street
Burlington, VT 05401

Conners Behavior Checklist
K. Conners
Multi-Health System, Inc.
908 Niagra Falls Blvd.
North Tonawanda, NY 14120-2060

Problem Behavior Checklist–Revised
R. Quay
Department of Psychology
University of Miami
Coral Gables, FL 33124

School Behavior Checklist
L. Miller
Western Psychological Services
12031 Wilshire Boulevard
Los Angeles, CA 90025

Walker Problem Behavior Identification– Revised (Grades P-6)
Western Psychological Services
12031 Wilshire Boulevard
Los Angeles, CA 90025

 Pointer Box 1-2

Sources for Social Skills Checklists

School Social Skills
L. Brown, D. Black, & J. Downs
Slosson Educational Publications
P.O. Box 280
East Aurora, NY 14052

Social Skills Rating System (SSRS)
F. Gresham & S. Elliott
American Guidance Services (AGS)
Publishers' Building
P.O. Box 99
Circle Pines, MN 55014-1796

Walker-McConnell Scale of Social Competence and Social Maladjustment
Pro-Ed Publishing Co.
5341 Industrial Oakes Boulevard
Austin, TX 78735

Teacher Compliance Probes

Compliance is simply defined as starting a requested behavior within a reasonably short period of time. Most students, when asked by a teacher, will respond to the request within ten seconds. However, Tough Kids delay, make excuses, and argue when given a request. They only comply approximately 40% or less of the time to teacher requests; the average student complies 80% of the time. A simple way to measure compliance is to systematically give a student a series (approximately ten requests) of common classroom tasks or behaviors over a week's period of time. Some common classroom requests are listed in How To Box 1-2.

The teacher should select needed requests from How To Box 1-2 and ask the student to do them. After each request, the teacher should wait ten

How To Box 1-2

Teacher Compliance Probes

The teacher gives a request, waits ten seconds, and marks "Yes" or "No" if the student started the requested behavior or did not. It is important (1) not to repeat the request, (2) not to reward the student with deals for compliance, (3) to act natural after the request, and (4) to wait the full ten seconds before acting or repeating the request.

Mark After Ten-Second Wait

1. Please sit down	Y	N
2. Line up at the door	Y	N
3. Put your books away	Y	N
4. Bring your assignment to my desk	Y	N
5. Be quiet	Y	N
6. Look at me	Y	N
7. Come here	Y	N
8. Get a pencil and paper out	Y	N
9. Write your name on the paper	Y	N
10. Get busy on your assignment	Y	N
11. Walk	Y	N
12. Look up front	Y	N
13. Come inside the room	Y	N
14. Sit down	Y	N
15. Go to your desk	Y	N
16. Put your books away	Y	N
17. Give me the pencil (or other object)	Y	N
18. Sit up	Y	N
19. Go to (place)	Y	N
20. Pick up the (item)	Y	N

SPECIFIC REQUESTS FROM YOUR CLASSROOM

21. _____	Y	N
22. _____	Y	N
23. _____	Y	N
24. _____	Y	N
25. _____	Y	N

At least ten different requests marked across a week are required to use the formula below:

Total Marked Yes ___ + Yes ___ + No___ X 100 =

Percent Compliant___%

Adapted with permission from Jesse (1989).

seconds for compliance. It is important not to interact with the student or repeat the request during this ten-second interval. Similarly, it is important to act natural when giving the request and not to offer rewards for compliance or scolding/lectures for noncompliance. Mark down on the sheet whether the student complies or does not comply to the request. Give at least ten (or up to 20) requests during the week and keep track of them on the request sheet. At the end of the week calculate the percentage of complied requests. If the percentage is 40% or less, then the student matches our definition of tough. Some students may be above 40% but well below the 80% for average students. These are generally easier students who should respond faster to the suggested procedures in this book.

Academic Assessment

Most teachers are familiar with standard academic achievement tests such as the **Stanford Achievement Test** or the **Peabody Individual Achievement Test–Revised**. These are good tests for obtaining a global academic measure of how well a student is performing by grade level or by chronological age. However, they are less well-suited for pinpointing specific academic deficits in particular curricula. To get a fine-grain analysis of a student's academic deficit, a curriculum-based measurement approach is much more functional. With a curriculum-based approach, a teacher selects a sample of academic probes from the student's actual curriculum. These academic probes represent critical skills necessary to master the curriculum. A student is administered the increasingly difficult probes until he/she fails a sequence. This is the point in the curriculum at which instruction should be started for the student.

Curriculum-based measurement is a practical means of determining instructional goals for Tough Kids. One distinct advantage is that it uses the student's actual curriculum materials.

Some excellent books on curriculum-based measurement are listed in Pointer Box 1-3.

 Pointer Box 1-3

Sources for Curriculum-Based Measurement

Academic Skills Problems: Direct Assessment and Intervention
E.S. Shapiro
Guilford Publications
72 Springs Street
NY, NY 10012

Curriculum-Based Evaluation for Special and Remedial Education
K.H. Howell & M.K. Morehead
Merrill Publishing Company
Columbus, OH 43216

Curriculum-Based Measurement: Assessing Special Children
M.R. Shinn (Editor)
Guilford Publications
72 Springs Street
NY, NY 10012

Observation Systems

Behavioral observation of a student is possibly one of the most accurate and valid of all the suggested assessment measures. In effect, behavioral observation is a collecting of a sample of the problem behavior in the setting in which it occurs. No recall from memory or judgement as to its severity is needed with behavioral observations. If the behavior occurs, it is simply recorded. However, difficulties with behavioral observation occur when observation systems are complicated and time consuming. In addition, few classroom observation systems have been standardized on groups of children and allow normative comparisons between students (such as the two standard deviation method comparison described above).

One simple behavioral observation approach that does allow normative comparisons is the **response discrepancy observation method**. The system is called response discrepancy because it allows a behavior discrepancy (difference) comparison between a target student (suspected Tough Kid) and the classroom peers. We suggest a teacher use the observation form given in How To Box 1-3.

This observation form is based on observing the on- and off-task behavior of a referred target student. The observer should be familiar with the on-task and off-task behavior codes listed on the bottom of the form. The basic class activity for a particular observation should be filled in (e.g., teacher directed whole class, teacher directed small group, independent seat work) plus the additional information on the form.

The actual observations are based on ten-second intervals (each box in the center of the form represents ten seconds) with 90 of these intervals included in the 15-minute observation period on which this form is based. The top interval box is for the referred target student and the bottom interval box is for a randomly selected, same sex peer. For each ten-second interval, the target student is observed along with a randomly

selected, same sex peer. If the target student is on-task for the entire ten-second interval, then an on-task code (i.e., a dot) is recorded. However, if the target student is off-task, the appropriate off-task code is recorded in the interval box. Only one off-task behavior is recorded

for each ten-second box. If more off-task behaviors occur, they are ignored until the next ten-second interval. The same recording process occurs for the same sex peer during the same ten-second interval for each box.

At the end of a 15-minute observation sample, a record of on- and off-task behavior is collected for the referred target student. The actual on-task percentage can be easily calculated for the 15-minute observation sample with the following equation: divide the number of on-task intervals by the total number of on- and off-task intervals, then multiply by one hundred. This equals the actual on-task percentage. Formula:

$$\frac{\# \ of \ on-task \ intervals}{\# \ of \ on-task + off-task \ intervals} \ x \ 100 = \_\_\% \ on-task.$$

In addition, a micro-norm or sample for on- and off-task behavior has been simultaneously collected on the same sex peers in the classroom and can be similarly calculated. This allows a comparison between our suspected Tough Kid and his/her peers. If our student is on-task 60% or less of the time and the peer's average is on-task 85% or more of the time, we know we have a distractible student. However, if both the suspected Tough Kid and the peer average for on-task behavior is below 60%, then the problem may be a more general classroom management problem.

How To Box 1-3

Behavior Observation Form

Target Student _____ M/F ___ Grade _____ Date _____

School _____ Teacher _____

Observer _____

Class Activity _____

Position ❑ Teacher directed whole class   ❑ Teacher directed small group   ❑ Independent work session

DIRECTIONS: Ten-second interval. Observe each student **once**; then record data. This is a partial interval recording. If possible, collect full 15 minutes under teacher directed or independent condition. If not, put a slash when classroom condition changes. **Classmates observed must be the same sex as the target student.**

Target
Student*

*Classmates of same sex.

Target
Student*

*Classmates of same sex.

Target
Student*

*Classmates of same sex.

Target
Student*

*Classmates of same sex.

Target
Student*

*Classmates of same sex.

NOTE: To observe class—begin with the first same sex student in row 1. Record each subsequent same sex student in following intervals. Data reflect an average of classroom behavior. **Skip unobservable students.**

ON-TASK CODES: Eye contact with teacher or task and performing the requested task.

OFF-TASK CODES:

- T = **Talking Out/Noise:** Inappropriate verbalization or making sounds with object, mouth, or body.
- O = **Out of Seat:** Student fully or partially out of assigned seat without teacher permission.
- I = **Inactive:** Student not engaged with assigned task and passively waiting, sitting, etc.
- N = **Noncompliance:** Breaking a classroom rule or not following teacher directions within 15 seconds.
- P = **Playing With Object:** Manipulating objects without teacher permission.
- + = **Positive Teacher Interaction:** One-on-one positive comment, smiling, touching, or gesture.
- - = **Negative Teacher Interaction:** One-on-one reprimend, implementing negative consequence, or negative gesture.

More Advanced Assessment Systems

Some new and very complete assessment systems for identifying Tough Kids have recently become available (see Pointer Box 1-4 for sources).

The *Systematic Screening for Behavior Disorders (SSBD)* is an efficient screening of entire schools for Tough Kids (Walker, Severson, Todis, & Block, 1987). This system uses a multigating approach in which each assessment step represents a gate through which a Tough Kid must pass before the next assessment (gate) can take place. In Gate One, all the teachers in a school rate their students from the most difficult to least difficult. In Gate Two, the three most difficult students listed in each classroom are then rated by the teacher against an established behavior checklist. If the students' behavior is severe enough as judged by the checklist ratings, then they are advanced to Gate Three assessment. In this gate, observations are made in the classroom and on the playground. If the observed behaviors are severe enough, the students are identified as disabled and a program is developed or they are referred for special services.

"Gate Crasher"

Pointer Box 1-4

Sources for Advanced Assessment Techniques

School Archival Record Search (SARS)
H. Walker, A. Block-Pedego, B. Todis, & H. Severson
Sopris West, Inc.
1140 Boston Avenue
Longmont, CO 80501

Systematic Screening for Behavior Disorders (SSBD)
H. Walker, H. Severson, B. Todis, & A. Block
Sopris West, Inc.
1140 Boston Avenue
Longmont, CO 80501

This approach is extremely thorough in identifying the most difficult students.

A unique approach in assessing Tough Kids is the newly developed *School Archival Records Search (SARS)* (Walker, Block-Pedego, Todis, & Severson, 1991). This system uses a student's cumulative school record or file to determine students who are at-risk, difficult students. The actual information and teacher comments from the student file are recorded and systematically rated. Since the information collected is generally a compilation of several teachers and school personnel, the cumulative record becomes a file of multiple measures by several different raters. Walker et al. (1991) have quantified such entries as school attendance, disciplinary contacts, within-school referrals for help, and others to accurately identify students who are noncompliant, disruptive, and aggressive. *SARS* allows actual normative comparisons (the two standard deviation comparisons–described above) to determine if a student's behavior is severe and truly tough. This approach can be particularly useful to teachers of new students who are transferring into their classroom and are suspected of being difficult.

Target Behaviors

Assessment information is valuable in identifying and determining the severity of problem behaviors in Tough Kids. However, the most important function of assessment information is to select and define behaviors for use with programs and interventions. All too often, assessment information is gathered and then ignored when behaviors are selected for change. The most severe behavior excesses and deficits from behavior checklists, observations, and probes should be selected as the target behaviors for change.

A good target behavior is a behavior that is:

- Observable—The behavior can actually be seen. It is not something that is underlying and assumed to be occurring.

- Measurable—The behavior can actually be measured (leaves a permanent product, like solutions to a math problem) or rated (on a behavior checklist, etc.).

- Well-defined—The behavior is defined objectively and simply so that two or more people can agree when the behavior occurs.

Poor target behaviors that are frequently selected for programs include such selections as the student has "a bad attitude," "poor sense of responsibility," "no internalized controls," "damaged self-esteem," etc. These all fail the tests of observability, measurability, and an objective definition. Workable target behaviors that parallel our definition of a Tough Kid are listed in Box 1-2.

Box 1-2

Target Behaviors for the Tough Kid

The Tough Kid:

(Noncompliance)

- Will follow a teacher's request within ten seconds
- Will follow posted classroom rules
- Will not argue
- Will not make excuses

(Aggression)

- Will not fight
- Will not be verbally abusive
- Will not destroy property
- Will not tantrum (scream, make threats, etc.)

(Self-Management Skills)

- Will follow directions
- Will exhibit problems solving skills (after training)
- Will explain the consequences of behaviors
- Will follow rules
- Will accept "No" for an answer

(Social Skills)

- Will learn to reward others
- Will explain and demonstrate cooperative behavior (after training)
- Will enter conversations appropriately
- Will demonstrate the skills of accepting negative feedback

(Academic Skills)

- Will finish assignments with 80% accuracy
- Will be on-task 85% of the time
- Will be on time to class
- Will not miss school
- Will hand in completed homework
- Will engage in peer tutoring
- Will be part of a cooperative learning team

Proactive Intervention Strategies

The first line of classroom intervention for Tough Kids should be preventative or proactive strategies. Proactive means that the **preplanned** strategy stops or interferes with most problem behaviors before they occur. The key to proactive or preventative strategies is to **anticipate** problem behaviors before they occur. It is much more difficult to remediate the problems caused by a Tough Kid than to prevent them. Once a teacher has lost the management tempo in a classroom and things are out of control, it is far more difficult to reestablish control.

Numerous strategies are available to teachers, and these strategies should be preplanned before school starts. These suggested strategies work for Tough Kids, and they also work for the average student to help enhance the overall quality of a classroom.

Classroom Rules–Don't Leave Home Without Them

Good classroom rules should be the backbone of any proactive strategy to reduce problem behaviors. Rules should form the nucleus of what type of behavior a teacher expects from all the students in a classroom. There should be a minimum expectation for behavior for every student in the classroom which the rules describe. All students should be expected to follow the rules including gifted and average students and Tough Kids. Once rule exceptions are made for special students, a double standard exists in a classroom and rules become worthless. How To Box 1-4 lists eight characteristics of good proactive rules.

It is important to make sure that students understand the resulting consequences (both positive and privilege loss) of the rules. During the first two weeks of school, a good exercise at the start of each day is to randomly select students to:

- read a posted rule,
- discuss and/or role play why the rule is important,
- explain what will happen if the rule is followed, and
- explain what will happen it the rule is not followed.

After the first two weeks, the teacher will want to watch for indications that the rules need to be reviewed again. This discussion and reading of rules is an appropriate time for any student to question why a rule exists. Any student should be allowed to question utility or fairness of a rule

"Rules X-Press Card"

How To Box 1-4

Characteristics of Good Proactive Rules

- Keep the number of rules to a **minimum**—about five rules for each classroom.

- Keep the wording of rules **simple**—pictures or icons depicting the rules help the understanding of younger students.

- Have the rules logically represent your **basic expectation** for a student's behavior in your classroom.

- Keep the wording **positive** if possible. Most rules can be stated in a positive manner; some rules cannot. However, the majority of classroom rules should be positive.

- Make your rules **specific**. The more ambiguous (i.e., open to several interpretations) the rules are, the more difficult they are to understand. Tough Kids can take advantage of nonspecific "loopholes" in poorly stated rules.

- Make your rules describe behavior that is **observable**. The behavior must be observable so that you can make an unequivocal decision as to whether or not the rule has been followed.

- Make your rules describe behavior that is **measurable**. That is, the behavior must be able to be counted or quantified in some way for monitoring purposes.

- Publicly post the rules in a prominent place in the classroom (e.g., in the front of the classroom, near the door). The lettering should be large and block-printed.

- Tie following the rules to **consequences**. You should spell out what happens positively if students follow the rules, and what they lose if they do not follow the rules. Frequently, teachers forget to state the positive consequences.

- Always include a **compliance rule**. You get the behavior that you post in rules. If you want to improve compliance in the classroom, include a rule such as "Do what your teachers asks immediately."

---

during this time. However, the teacher should make the final decision about the acceptability of a rule. It should not be a democratic decision by student vote. If a rule is overly stringent or unreasonable, then it can be changed by the teacher and a new rule can be constructed. However, rules should not be questioned by students at other times during the day, particularly when a rule has been broken. The beginning of the day is the time for rule discussion.

Teachers should select and post the core of the classroom rules **before** the first day of school (see Figure 1-3 for a sample format). The authors feel that student should not select their own rules for several reasons:

- When self-selecting rules, students tend to be overly punitive.

- Students often generate too many rules or nonspecific rules.

- Some Tough Kids feel they do not have to follow rules selected by other students: The authority of a teacher is needed.

The fine tuning of preselected rules can be done in the rule discussion during the first two weeks of school. It is also a good practice to periodically review the rules after holiday breaks,

Figure 1-3
Classroom Rules

Classroom Rules

_____

_____

_____

_____

_____

1 OBSERVABLE

2 MEASUREABLE

| 1 | 2 | 3 |

3 POSITIVE

4 ONLY FIVE

5 NO QUESTIONS

when several new students come into the classroom, or if there are extended periods of problem behaviors in the classroom. How To Box 1-5 gives several examples of inappropriate and appropriate rules.

Your Classroom Schedule—Down Time Causes Problems

The time not scheduled in a classroom is an open invitation to disruptive behavior. Scheduled academic learning time is critical to the academic success and appropriate classroom behavior of a Tough Kid. It is one of the basic proactive variables that is under teacher control. Academic learning time has three basic components: (1) the percentage of the day scheduled for academics (70% of the day), (2) on-task time of the student (85% on-task), and (3) success of the student once he/she is academically engaged (80% correct).

The total amount of time allocated in an instructional day is 100% (i.e., 6.5 hours in a typical classroom). The amount of this allocated time that should be scheduled for academic activities is approximately 70% or 5.2 hours of the instructional day. If the academic schedule (including transition times, recess, and lunch) is less than this amount, it is an enticement for disruptive behavior. To test your schedule, simply multiply the total hours the students are in school (allocated time) by 70%. The result is the minutes that should be scheduled for some type of academic activity (see the sample schedule in How To Box 1-6).

Many teachers feel overwhelmed at the thought of having students successfully academically engaged for 70% of the day. However, strategies such as peer tutoring and cooperative learning approaches make this a realistic goal. These strategies will be reviewed in the **Advanced Systems for Tough Kids** chapter.

How To Box 1-5

Examples of Inappropriate and Appropriate Rules

INAPPROPRIATE RULES

- Be responsible.
- Be a good citizen.
- Pay attention.
- Be ready to learn.
- Demonstrate respect for others.
- Respect others' rights.
- Respect authority.
- Treat school property appropriately.
- Do your best.
- Take care of your materials.
- Maintain appropriate behavior in the classroom.
- Be kind to others.
- Be polite.

PREFERRED RULE EXAMPLES

- Turn in completed assignments on time.
- Bring paper, pencil, and books to class.
- Sit in your seat unless you have permission to leave it.
- Do what your teacher asks immediately.
- Raise your hand and wait for permission to speak.
- Unless you have permission to speak, talk only about your work.
- Work when you are supposed to.
- Do not bother or hurt others.
- Walk, don't run, at all times in the classroom.
- Keep hands, feet, and objects to yourself.
- Bring books, notebooks, pens, and pencils to class.

How To Box 1-6

Example of a Classroom Schedule for Allocated Academic Time

A.M.

9:00 - 9:10	Attendance, lunch tickets, announcements
9:10 - 9:25	Peer tutor activity (reading or math)
9:25 - 10:10	Reading groups/independent practice and seatwork
10:10 - 10:25	Recess
10:25 - 11:10	Math instruction/independent practice (or Cooperative Learning Teams)
11:10 - 11:35	Spelling instruction/independent practice (or peer tutoring)
11:35 - 12:00	Expressive writing

P.M.

12:00 - 12:40	Lunch
12:40 - 1:20	Social studies
1:20 - 2:00	P.E. (M,W,F); art (T,TH)
2:00 - 2:15	Recess
2:15 - 2:55	Science
2:55 - 3:25	Social skills (M,W,F); music (T,TH)
3:25 - 3:30	Clean up and prepare for dismissal

Structuring Your Classroom Space

Two simple rules apply to Tough Kids when planning classroom space: (1) move them close to you, and (2) do not let Tough Kids sit together. These seem like common sense; however, these rules are constantly violated.

It seems that teachers feel uncomfortable about having an argumentative, disruptive, noncompliant student sit near them. These students are often placed in the back of the classroom (the out of sight, out of mind theory) or on the periphery of the classroom. This type of placement invites trouble. Tough Kids should be placed in the front of the classroom near the teacher. It should be noted that placing Tough

Kids close to you is not intended just to keep an eye on them. Instead, if they are close, they are more easily reinforced. At arms' length, it is convenient to socially reward these students in front of their peers and to ask them to help with basic classroom tasks (e.g., hand out papers, etc.).

"Having Tough Kids sit together is like disruptive behavior ability grouping."

Having Tough Kids sit together is like disruptive behavior ability grouping. Separate Tough Kids no matter what they promise or offer. When two or more Tough Kids sit together, they frequently reward each other for disruptive behavior. Some of this inappropriate encouragement is so subtle that it is difficult for a teacher to detect. If there is a group of Tough Kids in a classroom, have the most difficult sit up front and separate them by placing appropriate students near them.

Get Up and Move

Possibly one of the most effective and easy proactive strategies for teachers to use is simply to move around the classroom. The more time a teacher spends behind a desk, the more likely a Tough Kid will misbehave. Spend the time while students are at work walking around the class, and meet them at the door when they enter the classroom. A random walking approach, particularly where Tough Kids sit, is the most effective. Walking around permits a teacher to anticipate problems and to handle them before they get out of hand. It also allows a teacher to subtly reinforce students. For example, a simple touch on a shoulder, bending down and looking at a student's work, or pointing at a student's work and saying "Good job," are all easily done while walking around but difficult to do from behind a desk.

> **"The more time a teacher spends behind a desk, the more likely a Tough Kid will misbehave."**

Conduct a couple of simple tests. Keep track of the amount of time you actually spend behind your desk. For one week, try and cut this desk time in half and wander the classroom making positive comments. Look at your desk. Is it piled with material to occupy your time (e.g., books, objects, pictures, papers to grade)? Clean it off and walk. You will be amazed at the effect on classroom behavior.

Box 1-3 summarizes the proactive strategies teachers can employ to reduce problem behavior.

Box 1-3

Proactive Strategies for Teachers

Classroom Rules:

> *Don't leave home without them.*

Your Classroom Schedule:

> *Down time causes problems.*

Structuring Your Classroom Space:

> *Put Tough Kids near you.*

Get Up and Move:

> *Be a wandering reinforcer.*

Summary

All teachers will have a Tough Kid in their classroom sooner or later. The average is at least one or two of these students per year, and this average is not likely to go down. These students need not demoralize teachers or disrupt classrooms. It is important to remember that the behavioral excesses that cause these students to be perceived as difficult are present in all students. The only difference is that the **frequency** and **intensity** of aggression, noncompliance, arguing, and tantrum throwing is higher with Tough Kids. It is also critical to remember that **noncompliance** is the king-pin behavior around which these other behavioral excesses revolve. Reduce coercion and noncompliance in Tough Kids, and much of the arguing, aggression, and tantrum throwing will also be reduced.

Reducing noncompliance is only half of the battle with Tough Kids, however. The vast majority of Tough Kids have substantial behavioral deficits that interfere with adjustment. These students have significant deficits in basic academic, social, and self-management skills. Reducing coercion and noncompliance is only a temporary gain. If these students do not have their basic deficits remediated, then they will revert back to their excessive strategies to manage their environments. We cannot expect Tough Kids to do well in spite of feeling stupid, being rejected by their peers, or not having the basic skills to manage their own behaviors.

Three last points are critical if we hope to educate Tough Kids and enjoy the process. First, we **cannot drop our expectations** for these students. We must have the same high standard for academic and school behavior that we have for the average student. If we drop our expectations because these students come from poor backgrounds and are so deficit, then the research indicates they will fail. Research literature indicates that high expectations is one of the critical factors in effective schools.

Second, we must recognize that many of these students will not be "**cured**" during the time they are in our classrooms. The Tough Kid is **managed**. Accurate identification, proactive strategies, classroom interventions–all these procedures will make the educational environment work for the Tough Kid. It is not education's business to cure these students. No one, at this time, can do that. The business of education is to teach Tough Kids as many adaptive, academic, social, and self-management skills as possible. If we do that, then we immensely improve their chances for adjustment.

Third, these students must be educated in **positive classroom environments**. It is all too easy to use only punitive procedures with Tough Kids and then blame them for failing. Some reductive techniques may be necessary. However, unless basic positive approaches are used, we will lose the majority of these students. They will simply drop out of school, with an enormous cost to us as educators and to society as a whole. The next chapter outlines the basic positive procedures that should be used in classrooms that educate Tough Kids.

References

Achenbach, T.M. & Edelbrock, C. (1983). *Manual for the child behavior checklist and revised child behavior profile*. Burlington, VT: University of Vermont, Department of Psychiatry.

Gelfand, D.M., Jenson, W.R., & Drew, C. (1988). *Understanding childhood behavior disorders*. New York: Holt, Rinehart, and Winston.

Gresham, F. & Elliot, S. (1990). *Social skills rating system*. Circle Pines, MN: American Guidance Services.

Hofmeister, A. & Lubke, M. (1988). *Research into practice: Implementing effective teaching research*. Logan, UT: Utah State University, College of Education.

Jesse, V. (1989). *Compliance training and generalization effects using a compliance matrix and spinner system*. Unpublished doctoral dissertation, University of Utah, Salt Lake City, UT.

Patterson, G.R. (1982). *Coercive family process*. Eugene, OR: Castilia Publishing.

Skinner, B.F. (1953). *Science and human behavior*. New York: Macmillan.

U.S. Office of Education (1991, January). Focus group meeting on seriously emotionally disturbed students. Salt Lake City, UT.

Walker, H., Block-Pedego, A., Todis, B., & Severson, H. (1991). *School archival record search (SARS)*. Longmont, CO: Sopris West.

Walker, H., Severson, H., Todis, B., & Block, A. (1987). *Systematic screening for behavior disorders (SSBD)*. Longmont, CO: Sopris West.

Young, K.R., West, R.P., Smith, D.J., & Morgan, D.P. (1991). *Teaching self-management strategies to adolescents*. Longmont, CO: Sopris West.

Chapter 2

Unique Positive Procedures

"I tried that positive reinforcement stuff, but it didn't work!" So say many teachers of Tough Kids. However, it is an indisputable fact that behaviors which are supported and recognized are the ones which will increase. The trick is for the teacher to find ways to positively support and recognize Tough Kids' appropriate behavior in ways that are **meaningful to them**.

Obviously, if more teacher attention is given for inappropriate student behavior than for appropriate behavior, this is the behavior which will increase. With Tough Kids' teachers, this attention very often takes the form of excessive prompting, reminding, threatening, reprimanding, and verbal abuse, since this seems to come naturally when they attempt "pain control" of their own. Unfortunately, this pattern of teacher behavior in many, if not most, classrooms where teachers rely on human tendencies for management can actually cause the problem behaviors to increase rather than decrease. In these cases, arbitrary and capricious teacher attention focused on inappropriate behaviors is responsible for the maintenance and increase of undesired student behavior during the school year!

Thus, once teachers' classroom rules have been established at the beginning of the school year, the major driving force behind their classroom management must be the way they motivate and recognize students. It is only when Tough Kids view the classroom as a positive place to be that they will not need to practice "pain control" and will want to be in the classroom. Tough Kids' teachers must find unique and interesting ways to consistently provide motivation and recognition to their students for exhibiting the behaviors they desire to increase. Not only will they be able to affect behavior changes in the students, but the classroom will simply be a more positive place for them to be as well. If adequate motivation and recognition are not in place, no classroom management plan will **ever** be effective.

"Pain Control"

Positive Strategies

Positive Reinforcement

First a word about positive reinforcement. Positive reinforcement involves the contingent presentation of something valued or desired by the student. Mind you, this may not be the same thing that the teacher thinks the student values or desires, or that the teacher thinks the student **should** value or desire. This "something" the student values is given immediately **after** the desired behavior and results in an increase in the behavior.

Some everyday examples include the following:

Every day that Ellen finishes her reading assignment on time, Mrs. Farmer allows her to take sports equipment out at recess. If Ellen enjoys using the equipment at recess, she is likely to continue finishing her assignments on time.

"Wanna play hockey?"

When Kenny remembers to raise his hand before speaking in class, Mr. Orton awards a point to the class toward a class party. Because Kenny's peers now encourage him to remember to raise his hand and because he enjoys parties, Kenny is likely to remember to raise his hand in Mr. Orton's class.

While the above examples demonstrate the appropriate use of positive reinforcement for increasing desired student behavior, Tough Kids' teachers often inadvertently provide positive reinforcement for behaviors they do **not** wish to see increase.

> **"If the behavior increases, reinforcement has occurred. If it does not, what was provided was not reinforcing to the Tough Kid."**

Some examples include:

Every time Jessica is out of her seat, Mrs. Harper tells her to sit down. Mrs. Harper cannot understand why it seems that Jessica is out of her seat more than ever.

Mr. White sends Darrin out in the hall to sit on a chair because of disruptive behavior in the classroom. Darrin talks to other students and adults who pass by him, in addition to helping himself to candy he finds in the pocket of another student's coat. Mr. White finds that Darrin is disruptive again soon after he is permitted to return to the classroom.

In both of these situations, students received attention from others as a result of their inappropriate behavior. Many students, like Jessica, find even negative attention from the teacher reinforcing, particularly in classrooms where their appropriate behavior is not recognized or rewarded. By definition, if the Tough Kid's behavior increases, it has been reinforced. This is true even if the teacher thought he/she was punishing the student (see Box 2-1).

BOX 2-1

Positive Reinforcement, Negative Reinforcement, and Punishment

It is all too easy to confuse positive reinforcement, negative reinforcement, and punishment. **Both** positive and negative reinforcement **increase** behavior, while punishment **decreases** it.

Positive reinforcement is said to occur when something a student desires is presented after appropriate behavior has been exhibited.

> • Example: *Colby can now earn up to ten points for completing his reading workbook assignment correctly. The points can be exchanged for dinosaur stickers. Because Colby enjoys the stickers he can earn, the accuracy of his assignments has increased.*

Negative reinforcement is said to occur when students engage in particular behavior to **avoid** or **escape** something they dislike.

> • Example: *Jennifer's truant behavior increases to avoid an English class in which she is unable to do the work.*

> • Example: *Howard hurries and finishes his math assignment so he will not be kept in from recess to complete it.*

Punishment is said to occur when something the student does not like or wishes to avoid is applied after the behavior has occurred, resulting in a **decrease** in the behavior.

> • Example: *Every time John skips school, he is required to make up the missed time in an after-school detention. Because he dislikes after-school detention so much, the skipping stops.*

Thus, if the teacher wishes to increase the Tough Kid's (appropriate) behavior and provides what he/she deems to be positive reinforcement after the desired behavior has been exhibited, the results of this action must be examined. If the behavior increases, reinforcement has occurred. If it does not, what was provided was not reinforcing to the Tough Kid.

In order to determine that desired behavior has actually increased, a simple monitoring system will need to be established. If the behavior is not monitored, it is almost impossible to tell if appropriate behavior is increasing or not. If it is not, the teacher will want to know that relatively soon, so that neither the teacher's nor the Tough Kid's time and effort are wasted with an ineffective strategy.

Concerns With Positive Reinforcement

Some teachers think that it is wrong to use positive reinforcement. They believe that Tough Kids should just exhibit appropriate behavior because it is the responsible thing to do. They may view reinforcement as a crutch or bribe. These concerns deserve examination.

First of all, many regular students exhibit appropriate behavior because it is the responsible and "right" thing to do. Even so, they still need positive reinforcement. Likewise, not very many Tough Kids' teachers would continue to work if they did not receive paychecks. Similarly, **all** students need legitimate reinforcement. Positive reinforcement is no more a crutch

> **"Positive reinforcement is no more a crutch for students than money, credit cards, and public recognition are crutches for adults."**

for students than money, credit cards, and public recognition are crutches for adults.

As far as the bribery issue goes, we can agree that teachers should not use bribery with **any** student. However, appropriately administered positive reinforcement is not a bribe. Webster's dictionary defines a bribe as an inducement for an illegal or unethical act. Of course, a teacher would never do anything illegal or unethical with a student.

Another way of viewing a bribe is the giving of a reward to an individual to stop an inappropriate behavior or misbehavior. Examples of bribes can be seen every day in the grocery store when a mother gives her child a cookie if the child stops crying or throwing a tantrum. This use of a reward is never appropriate for any individual. Proper positive reinforcement is given only after an **appropriate** behavior to increase or maintain that behavior.

Some teachers also believe that giving positive reinforcement takes too much time or is not sincere and genuine. A feeling of spontaneity and genuineness comes only with practice. The teacher who believes that giving routine reinforcement to students takes too much time or detracts from more important tasks is on the wrong track. With this attitude, classroom management will never be effective, especially with Tough Kids, and the teacher can count on spending a great deal of time and effort dealing with increased student misbehavior. Nothing is more important than positively reinforcing students for appropriate behavior! This is even more critical with Tough Kids than with other students.

Antecedent Strategies

An antecedent strategy is one which comes **before** a behavior and increases or maintains it. Antecedent strategies increase Tough Kids' motivation and encourage them to exhibit desired behavior. Use of antecedent strategies may be viewed as "setting the stage" for appropriate behavior to occur. When it is possible to use antecedent strategies it is desirable to do so, rather than waiting for the appropriate behavior to occur and then reinforcing it.

The effectiveness of antecedent strategies is not limited to education and has gained widespread attention in the business world in recent years. Ways to help the worker work more effectively is a hot topic in many arenas. More and more companies are recognizing and rewarding employees with performance incentives. The logic in creating incentive and recognition programs for employees is inescapable. Formal and informal research both demonstrate that people who feel appreciated hustle more, treat customers better and in general provide a higher level of service which, in turn, brings customers back (Hequet, 1990).

In the business world, effective motivators can include merchandise, time off with pay, recognition banquets, training to enhance skills or build new ones, company picnics, tickets to ball games, and money. Box 2-2 lists examples of positive antecedent strategies for **classroom** use.

BOX 2-2

Positive Antecedent Strategies

Encouragement

- "I know you can do this!"
- "Let's see if you can do as well as you did yesterday."
- "Give it a try!"

Structuring Incentives

- "Students who are in their seats when the bell rings can choose where they sit tomorrow."
- "When the class has accumulated five days with no tardies, we'll have a 20-minute party at the end of class."
- "Students who have not been sent to the office or had a phone call home for inappropriate behavior will be eligible for our raffle drawing."
- "I'm giving each of you a 20%-off bonus card this morning. Anyone who earns 80 or more points by 3:00 P.M. can use the bonus card in the class store."

Hype

- "Wow! I've got a ten minute free time coupon today for anyone earning 90% or better on the quiz. I know a lot of you are anxious to try out our new video game during free time. Everyone I know who has tried it says it's the best one on the market! Let's see who can try it out first. It's really great!"
- "Don't forget we'll be having a raffle drawing on the last day of school for everyone who has earned it. The prizes are super. You're going to want to be there! You've got a great chance of winning something. Just remember to follow the rules."

Relating Academic Accomplishments to Outcomes

- "Everyone who passes the mastery test can skip study hall and take an extra 15 minutes recess."
- "Students who have all their work caught up will be eligible to work as peer tutors in Mrs. Stock's second grade class."
- "Students who have a B+ average or better in reading will receive an award at the Parents' Night Assembly."

Motivation and Encouragement

Motivating and encouraging desired performance is much the same in the classroom as it is in the business world. The steps are quite simple:

1. Tell students what you want them to do (and make certain they understand it).

2. Tell them what will happen if they do what you want them to do.

3. When students do what you want them to do, give them **immediate** positive feedback in ways that are direct and meaningful to them.

The key word in Step Three is the word "immediate." If recognition is delayed until the end of the term or the school year, it might as well not be given at all. For most students (and employees), this long of a delay translates into ineffective or essentially meaningless recognition. Recognition systems should be ongoing in the classroom all of the time. In essence, recognition should consist of the teacher's ongoing dialogue with the students and orchestration of classroom climate for learning and good citizenship. For many students, recognition of desired performance can be more powerful than a tangible reward.

The proactive strategies detailed in Chapter One are also considered antecedent strategies. Classroom desk arrangement, specification of expectations and rules, daily schedule, appropriate and motivating curriculum, appropriate instructional pacing, adequate supervision, etc., all help to prevent behavior problems from occurring in the first place. The teacher will always want to assess if he/she has adequately addressed antecedent strategies before proceeding with more intrusive interventions for Tough Kids.

Effective Use of Positive Reinforcement

A critical element in effective classroom management with Tough Kids is determining the positive reinforcement that will be made available to them **contingent** upon their appropriate behavior. Careful selection and use of positive reinforcement is essential, since the teacher will rely heavily on positive reinforcement to increase appropriate behavior. Cautions to keep in mind when selecting and using positive reinforcement are listed in How To Box 2-1.

Two categories of positive reinforcement must be examined: (1) natural reinforcement readily available within the classroom or school or that can be made available as an ongoing part of the school program, and (2) other reinforcement to which the teacher has access and can make available. In identifying either type of positive reinforcement, creativity is critical!

Natural Positive Reinforcement

Many forms of natural positive reinforcement are available in school settings if one only looks for them. Many times teachers have become so used to allowing students noncontingent access to available natural positive reinforcement that they forget it is there—and available for use as

powerful contingent reinforcement, based on appropriate behavior. Box 2-3 gives examples of potential natural positive reinforcement that a teacher may want to use.

A teacher dealing with Tough Kids must consider all natural reinforcement he/she can think of that is already available within the classroom or school. For example, one teacher of Tough Kids we know was befriended by the elderly, Italian school custodian, who reaped mountains of produce from his large vegetable garden each fall. Nearly every day, in his attempts to be "helpful," he would bring her armloads of giant zucchinis for the class. She began by planning cooking projects using zucchinis as rewards for the class. Once zucchini cookies, bread and dip had been exhausted, she went on to use them in art projects, even having students create decorative centerpieces and bookends from the seemingly never ending supply of the green vegetable. Finally, when one day the custodian proudly rolled a large dolly cart containing at least two dozen gargantuan zucchinis into her classroom, she was at her wits' end. On the spur of the moment and with a great deal of fanfare, she announced to the class that anyone who had earned 90 or more out of a possible 100 behavior points for the day would receive two zucchinis to take home, and those with at least 80 points would receive one! As points were tallied, the

How To Box 2-1

Cautions in Selecting and Using Positive Reinforcement

1. Select reinforcement which is age appropriate.

2. Use "natural" reinforcement whenever it is effective.

3. Use reinforcement appropriate to the student's level of functioning. (e.g., Don't send a student for unsupervised free time in the library when he/she usually gets in trouble in the library even when he/she is directly supervised.)

4. Make certain you have parental and administrative support for the reinforcement you plan to use.

5. Avoid partial praise statements such as, "I'm glad you finished your work—finally!"

6. Always make the most of opportunities to reinforce appropriate behavior.

7. Be genuinely polite and courteous to Tough Kids at all times and demonstrate concern and interest towards them. Learn to stay calm.

8. Do not confuse positive reinforcement or privileges with a student's basic rights. (e.g., Depriving a student of lunch, reasonable access to the bathroom or clothing, or a telephone call home is probably illegal. It is also not appropriate to deprive students of their rights and then have them earn them back under the guise of reinforcement.)

teacher had each student come forward to accept the earned zucchinis as the class applauded. Afterwards, the teacher got a good laugh with her colleagues over the use of her novel reinforcement and the probable comments in the homes of her students that evening as they explained how they had earned their zucchinis with good behavior.

Being familiar with the students is, of course, very helpful in determining what is likely to be positively reinforcing to them. The teacher who knows his/her students fairly well has had opportunities to observe them to see what they like to do, what they are willing to work for, and to ask them what they like. Parents, former teachers, and experience with similar students can provide a list with which to begin. Changes can be made as appropriate later on.

For those Tough Kids whose appropriate behavior is extremely limited, natural positive reinforcement may not be powerful enough initially to increase desired behavior. More importantly, the teacher may be unable to provide access to much of the available natural reinforcement if the student's behavior is too unstable or inappropriate to allow his/her access to the environment where it can be delivered. For example, a physically and verbally abusive student would not be sent to serve as a lunchroom worker or to deliver office messages. For these students the teacher needs to identify other powerful reinforcement that can be made available in the classroom and which the teacher is willing to provide initially, until behavior is under control enough for the student to access more natural reinforcement. Other reinforcement may take several forms.

Box 2-3

Suggestions for Natural Positive Reinforcement

- Access to lunchroom snack machines (student supplies money)
- Attend school dances
- Attend school assemblies
- Be first in line (to anything)
- Be team captain
- Care for class pets
- Choose activity or game for class
- Class field trips
- Decorate the classroom
- Eat lunch in cafeteria rather than in classroom
- Extra portion at lunch
- Extra P.E., recess, or break time

- Free time to use specific equipment/supplies
- Give the student a place to display work
- Have the use of a school locker
- Help custodian
- Omit certain assignments
- Pass out paper
- Run errands
- Run film projector or video player for class
- Serve as class or office messenger or aide
- Sharpen class pencils
- Sit at teacher's desk for a specified period
- Sit by a friend

- Time with a favorite adult or peer
- Tutor in class, or with younger students
- Use of playground or P.E. equipment
- Use of class "walkman" or tape recorder
- Use of magic markers and/or art supplies
- Visit the principal (prearranged)
- Visit the school library (individual or group)
- Water class plants
- Work as a lunchroom server
- Write on chalkboard (regular or colored chalk)

Edible Reinforcement

This refers to the providing of foods students like to eat. Generally, edible reinforcement is equally effective with both elementary and secondary populations. Some common forms of edible reinforcement are candy, ice cream, pop, pizza, french fries, pretzels, chips, and juice. Interestingly, in a recent study of five- to twelve-year old Tough Kids, their highest rated edible reinforcer was french fries (Dewhurst & Cautela, 1980).

It should be noted that some students with severe disabilities like to eat nonnutritive substances such as cigarette butts, buttons, rocks, dirt, and chalk. It would be erroneous to assume that these items do not serve as reinforcement for the students who eat them. If the substance that a student eats increases or maintains a behavior, then it serves as reinforcement. However, for most Tough Kids it is not difficult to identify appropriate, edible reinforcement.

The same teacher who convinced her junior high class that it was great to earn zucchinis as a reward also had them believing that earning a "Wally's donut" was sheer ecstasy. When she planned to make Wally's donuts available as a reinforcement, she began ahead of time announcing what day she would be bringing them and what was needed to earn one. She would

"Wally's Donuts"

describe them in juicy detail until the students were virtually drooling. On the day she brought them she would display them and again remind students just how fabulous they were. This teacher's students would do almost anything to earn a Wally's donut by the time she was finished with her "marketing" plan.

Material Reinforcement

Earning material items can be highly reinforcing for Tough Kids. Material reinforcement consists of the delivery of some type of tangible item which will increase or maintain behavior. Five-to twelve-year old Tough Kids recently rated stickers as their most-preferred nonedible reinforcers (Dewhurst & Cautela, 1980). Box 2-4 lists suggestions for tangible items that Tough Kids' teachers have effectively used for reinforcement.

Pointer Box 2-1 lists suggestions of places to find novel reinforcers.

Generally, edible and material reinforcement are more useful than natural reinforcement for Tough Kids who initially require reinforcement that is immediate, more frequent, and may be delivered in smaller amounts at a time. For ex-

ample, a Tough Kid may be required to work appropriately for a ten minute block of time to earn two minutes use of a hand-held video game. The specific Tough Kids the teacher is working with will determine the reinforcement form, amount, and how often it must be delivered to be effective. In addition to the types of reinforcement already explained, there is one more which is probably the most important form of reinforcement for all human beings, covered below.

Social Reinforcement

A smile, a comment on a job well done, and a compliment are all examples of social reinforcement. Social reinforcement is any social behavior by the teacher that increases or maintains student behavior. Since many Tough Kids are socially unskilled and have difficulty interacting with others, they may be starved for social reinforcement. Many of the annoying and aggravating behaviors of Tough Kids are also linked to this social reinforcement deprivation. Attention (even negative attention) from another person can serve as extremely powerful reinforcement. Unfortunately, many teachers working with Tough Kids do not deliver anywhere near the

---

Box 2-4

Suggestions for Material Reinforcement

- Address book
- Art supplies
- Badges
- Ball
- Balloons
- Bean bags
- Book
- Bookmark
- Bubble blowing set
- Calendar
- Audio cassette tapes
- Chalk
- Clay or play dough
- Colored paper
- Coloring books
- Comics
- Cosmetics

- Crayons
- Eraser
- Games
- Good Student certificates
- Grab-Bag: toys, candy, decals
- Hackey Sack
- Jacks
- Jewelry
- Jump rope
- Key chains
- Magic markers
- Marbles
- Miniature cars
- Model kits
- New pencil
- Paintbrushes/paints
- Play money

- Positive note home
- Positive phone call home
- Posters
- Puzzles
- Real money
- Rings
- School supplies
- Seasonal cards
- Self-stick skin tattoos
- Stickers
- Stuffed animals
- Surprise treats or rewards (random)
- Toiletries
- Toys
- Wax lips and teeth
- Yo-yo

---

level of social reinforcement that effective classroom management for these students requires.

Assessing and Selecting Reinforcement

It is a mistake for teachers to assume that they automatically know what will serve as reinforcement for Tough Kids. The rule of thumb for teachers is to try the potential reinforcer; if the behavior increases, then it is reinforcement. Many teachers assume that if they like something, or similar students like something, then a particular Tough Kid will also find that something reinforcing.

It is not unusual to hear a teacher say, "I tried positive reinforcement, but it didn't work!" Re-

member, if the behavior did not actually increase, there was no positive reinforcement. There are several practical steps in assessing potential reinforcement for Tough Kids.

First, it is important to **watch** and **try**. By watching Tough Kids, it is possible to determine what they like to do. The activities that students engage in are generally reinforcing. Students can be observed during free time, transition times, leisure time, and even class time. The activity the student voluntarily engages in or the item frequently asked for are likely to be reinforcing.

Examples:

In one junior high class of Tough Kids, several of the students would always rush to use the snack machines in the lunchroom. When the teacher observed how popular this activity was, she made the use of the machines (with the students' own money)

Pointer Box 2-1

Where to Find Novel Reinforcers

Interesting and unique reinforcers may be found in a variety of places. Some of the more popular places with examples of what they offer are listed below:

Costume Shops

- costume accessories
- make-up
- masks
- wigs

Flea Markets and Teachers' Attics/Basements

- old clothes for "dress up"
- sports equipment
- toys, books, comic books, games

Magic or Trick Shop

- "mind bender" puzzles and games
- simple magic tricks

Novelty Stores

- artificial scars
- broken glass decals
- disappearing ink
- fake melted ice cream bar
- flavored toothpicks
- hand buzzer
- plastic ants
- plastic ice cube with fly in it
- rubber vomit

contingent upon the earning of a prespecified number of points for appropriate behavior that day.

Mrs. King noticed that Sherry, Ben, and Michael spent their free time coloring with magic markers on detailed posters which she had made available. Once she saw how popular the activity was, she began to make the use of the markers contingent upon appropriate behavior. For each instructional session in which students earned eight out of ten possible behavior points, they could color with markers on their posters for three minutes.

Asking is also an important step in assessing reinforcers. While in some cases students may have a hard time thinking of things they would like to earn, many students will be able to give the teacher ideas. It is certainly worth the teacher's time to simply ask the student what he/she would like to earn. Above all, the Tough Kid's teacher must learn to **think** like a Tough Kid in order to select effective reinforcement.

Reinforcer checklists are another means of determining effective reinforcement for individual students. The checklists contain lists of potential reinforcers which are generally listed according to categories such as edible, material, social, etc. A reinforcer checklist may be teacher-made or purchased commercially (Cautela & Brion-Meisels, 1979; Gelfand & Hartmann, 1975; Clement & Richard, 1976). Students are simply asked to check the items which they would like to earn. For students who cannot read, the teacher can interview the student and read the lists to him/her, marking the selections.

A variation of a reinforcer checklist is a **reinforcer menu** (see Figure 2-1). This approach may be particularly useful with students who have difficulty communicating their needs and wants. A menu is simply a list of pictures (cut from magazines or drawn) of known reinforcers that the student likes. In selecting a reinforcer, the student has only to point to the item of choice. The items can be changed or updated peri-

Figure 2-1
Reinforcer Menu

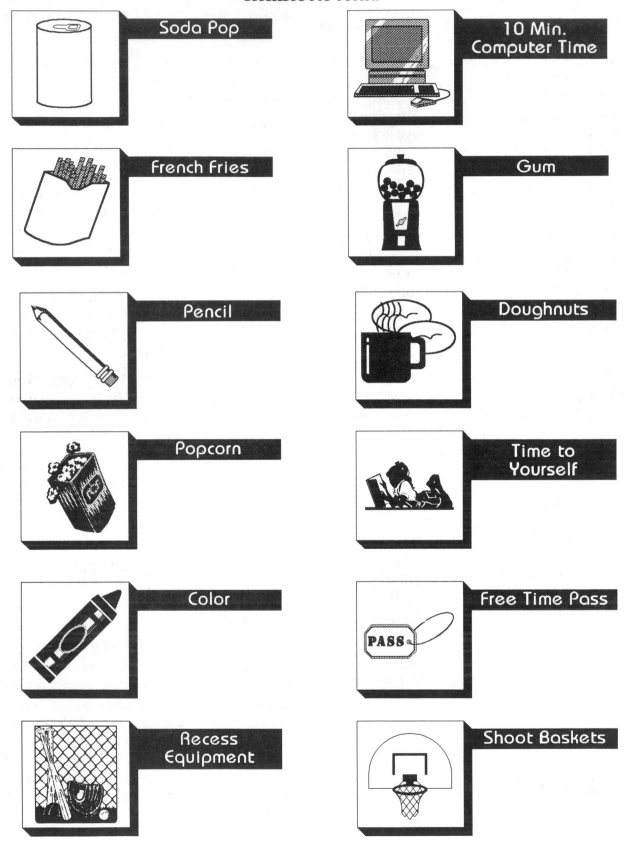

odically. Mystery (denoted as ???) or surprise items may also be included on the menu.

Reinforcement sampling is another assessment technique to determine effective reinforcers. With reinforcement sampling, a number of potential reinforcers are displayed for a limited period of time (e.g. an hour, a day, etc.) so that students can see them and access them. The teacher simply observes what types of reinforcers students sample (food, toys, activities) during this time and writes them down. Selected reinforcers can then be made into a reinforcement menu.

One mistake that teachers of Tough Kids sometimes make is to go ahead and give students the reinforcer first, after extracting a promise that they will do what it is they are supposed to do. For example, Shane's teacher may tell him he may go on the class field trip if he promises not to get in any fights the rest of the week.

Grandma's Law, also known as the **Premack Principle**, is a rule about reinforcement that grandmothers seem to have known about and

used since the beginning of time (Premack, 1959). According to this principle, the reinforcer is always given **after** the desired behavior and never before. For example:

Grandma told Jeannie, "Eat your liver and onions first and then you may have cookies and ice cream."

Kenny's teacher, Ms. Young, said, "After you finish your work, you may go out to recess."

Grandma's Law is common sense. Do this . . . and then I will give you what you want. Teachers frequently turn the principle around, however, rendering what they considered to be reinforcement ineffective. For example:

Grandma told Jeannie, "OK, go ahead and eat your cookies and ice cream first. But I want you to promise me that you will then eat your liver and onions."

Kenny's teacher, Ms. Young, said, "I'm going to go ahead and let you go out to recess if you will be sure to finish your work as soon as you come back in."

These examples typify common mistakes. In these situations, the desired behaviors (e.g., chores, school work, etc.) usually do not occur.

"But Doctor, Nothing Reinforces My Student!"

While it is more difficult to find effective reinforcers for some students than others, there is **always** something that will reinforce a student. The only time this will not be true is if the student is dead! There is always some edible, natural, material or social reinforcer that will work—the trick is to find it (see Box 2-5). Once reinforcers have been selected, the teacher may have to improve the effectiveness of the reinforcers to make them work.

"Grandma's Law"

Box 2-5

The Golden Rule for Selecting Reinforcers

There is a **Golden Rule** for selecting reinforcers. If it is not followed, the reinforcers generally do not work. The Golden Rule states that any selected reinforcers should not cost a lot of **money**, should not take a lot of staff **time**, and should be **natural**, whenever possible.

Anyone can think of expensive, highly artificial or time consuming reinforcers. The problem is that the reinforcers will not be used consistently or frequently under these circumstances. There are thousands of reinforcers which are not too costly in terms of time and money and many which are also natural. Selecting reinforcers is a great time for the Tough Kids' teacher to exercise creativity!

Variables That Make Reinforcers Effective

There is a simple set of rules to follow to make reinforcers more effective. These rules are called **IFEED-AV** strategies in which each letter stands for a strategy that makes a reinforcer more effective. The IFEED-AV rules are described in How To Box 2-2.

Taking a chance or not being able to predict the reinforcement that will be earned is exciting for a student, particularly if there is a chance of receiving a bigger reinforcer. Stores frequently capitalize on this strategy in their promotional campaigns to get people to patronize their businesses. For example, a fast food restaurant may offer a chance for a trip to Hawaii along with lots of chances to win a small coke or an order of french fries if a meal is bought there. A similar strategy may be used very effectively with Tough Kids through the use of "spinners" and "grab bags." These strategies will be described in detail later in this chapter.

In addition to the IFEED-AV rules, there are other guidelines to keep in mind for enhancing reinforcer effectiveness. First, **deprivation** makes students want a reinforcer more. In other words, if they have not just had access to the reinforcer, it is much more likely to be an effective reinforcer. Hunger is a good example of this. If an individual has not eaten for several hours, food will serve as a more powerful reinforcer than right after a large meal. However, it is important to remember that students must never be deprived of the essentials to which they have a right (e.g. food, water, bathroom, etc.).

The **magnitude** of the reinforcer is another variable that affects the potency of a reinforcer. Tough Kids are more likely to work for a larger reward than for a smaller one. However, this is true only up to a point. If the reinforcer is too large, the student will quickly tire of it. If it is too small, the student may become frustrated and stop performing. It is very important to select just the right amount of reinforcer

IFEED-AV Rules

Immediately: The "I" stands for reinforcing the student immediately. The longer the teacher waits to reinforce a student, the less effective the reinforcer will be. This is particularly true of younger students or students with severe disabilities. For example, reinforcer effectiveness will be limited if the student has to wait until the end of the week to receive it.

Frequently: The "F" stands for frequently reinforcing a student. It is especially important to frequently reinforce when a student is learning a new behavior or skill. If reinforcers are not given frequently enough, the student may not produce enough of a new behavior for it to become well established. The standard rule is three or four positive reinforcers for every one negative consequence (including negative verbal comments) the teacher delivers. If, in the beginning, there is a great deal of inappropriate behavior to which the teacher must attend, positive reinforcement and recognition of appropriate behavior must be increased accordingly to maintain the desired three or four positives to each negative. The reinforcer can be a simple social reinforcer such as, "Good job. You finished your math assignment."

Enthusiasm: The first "E" stands for enthusiasm in the delivery of the reinforcer. It is easy to simply hand an edible reinforcer to a student; it takes more effort to pair it with an enthusiastic comment. Modulation in the voice and excitement with a congratulatory air conveys that the student has done something important. For most teachers, this seems artificial at first. However, with practice enthusiasm makes the difference between a reinforcer delivered in a drab, uninteresting way to one that indicates that something important has taken place in which the teacher is interested.

Eye Contact: It is also important for the teacher to look the student in the eyes when giving a reinforcer, even if the student is not looking at him/her. Like enthusiasm, eye contact suggests that a student is special and has the teacher's undivided attention. Over time, eye contact may become reinforcing in and of itself.

Describe the Behavior: "D" stands for describing the behavior that is being reinforced. The younger the student or the more severely disabled, the more important it is to describe the appropriate behavior that is being reinforced. Teachers often assume that students know what it is they are doing right that has resulted in the delivery of reinforcement. However, this is often not the case. The student may not know why reinforcement is being delivered or think that it is being delivered for some behavior other than what the teacher intended to reinforce. Even if the student does know what behavior is being reinforced, describing it is important.

For one thing, describing the behavior highlights and emphasizes the behavior the teacher wishes to reinforce. Second, if the behavior has several steps, describing it helps to review the specific expectations for the student. An example is, "Wow, you got yourself dressed—look at you! You have your socks on, your shoes are laced, your pants are on with a belt, and your shirt has all the buttons fastened and is tucked in." This is much more effective than saying, "Good dressing."

Anticipation: Building excitement and anticipation for the earning of a reinforcer can motivate students to do their very best. The more "hype" the teacher uses, the more excited students become to earn the reinforcer. Presenting the potential reinforcer in a "mysterious" way will also build anticipation.

Variety: Just like adults, students, and particularly Tough Kids, get tired of the same things. A certain reinforcer may be highly desired, but after repeated exposure, it loses its effectiveness. It is easy to get caught up in giving students the same old reinforcers time and time again. However, variety is the spice of life for nondisabled and disabled alike. Generally, when teachers are asked why they do not vary their reinforcers, they indicate that it worked very well once. It is necessary to change reinforcers frequently to make the reinforcement more effective.

(whether food, money, activities, or praise) to keep the Tough Kid motivated.

The **schedule** of delivery of a reinforcer is another important effectiveness variable. By schedule we mean the amount of the desired behavior that is required before the reinforcer is given. When a student is first learning a new behavior, **continuous reinforcement** is best. This means that after every correct response, a reinforcer is given. Likewise, when a student is first learning a complex task, it is important to reinforce him/her after every correct step. However, once the student has learned the correct behavior or steps, then **intermittent reinforcement** is preferable. For example, in using intermittent reinforcement, the teacher might reinforce after every third (or some other number) math problem completed correctly. This is called a **fixed schedule of reinforcement** because the teacher has fixed the requirement for reinforcement at three.

This fixed schedule has the advantage that the student will not tire of the reinforcer as quickly as with a continuous reinforcement schedule. The disadvantage is that some students will stop working right after the reinforcement is given and won't start back to work immediately. If this is a problem, it can be remedied by switching to what is called a **variable schedule of reinforcement**. With a variable schedule, for example, on the average every third response (or some other number) might be reinforced. However, the important difference here is the term **average**. Sometimes the teacher might reinforce the student after seven correct responses, then three responses, then four responses, then ten responses, then one response. The Tough Kid can never be sure he/she will not be reinforced immediately after he/she gives the next correct response, because the response requirement is random and only the average is fixed. Because of this uncertainty, variable reinforcement is usually very effective for use with Tough Kids.

Fading

Some teachers criticize the use of positive reinforcement, because they believe students will become too dependent on reinforcement and will always expect to receive it for everything they do. They assume that all positive reinforcement is artificial and that students should behave appropriately because it is the responsible thing to do.

This reasoning has two basic flaws. First, our students are Tough Kids who may need extra inducements to get them to even begin to exhibit desired behavior. Without reinforcement, there is little motivation for these students to change their behavior. Second, it is erroneous to believe that most people work without some type of reinforcer. As we've already mentioned, few teachers (and other employees) would show up at work if paychecks were not distributed periodically.

Ideally, the teacher gets the Tough Kid started using potent and even artificial reinforcers, if necessary. He/she will then reduce the amount of reinforcement over time, requiring more and more of the appropriate behavior, and gradually shift to more natural rewards. This reduction in reinforcers is called **fading**. How To Box 2-3 outlines the steps to use for fading.

Fading frequently fails when reinforcement is stopped too quickly or is not paired with social praise. Through this pairing, the social praise will eventually assume the reinforcing qualities of the reinforcement with which it is paired. Gradually the reinforcement is reduced, leaving the social praise as the major rein-

> **"... few teachers ... would show up at work if paychecks were not distributed periodically."**

Steps for Fading Reinforcement

1. Provide reinforcement to the student for desired performance. Continuous reinforcement is usually desirable until the student is performing at an acceptable level.

2. Always pair the delivery of the reinforcement with specific social reinforcement (e.g., "I like the way you lined up without pushing or shoving.").

3. Gradually move from a continuous reinforcement schedule to an intermittent schedule (either fixed or variable).

4. As reinforcement becomes more intermittent, gradually move from artificial reinforcement to more natural reinforcement.

5. Continue to use social reinforcement generously.

forcer of the appropriate behavior. It is never desirable to completely fade out social praise.

Ideally, a teacher's goal is to fade all students from more artificial forms of reinforcement. However, many Tough Kids with long-standing histories of severe behavior problems may require some form of intermittent reinforcement program for a long period of time, perhaps for several years. The effort required for the teacher to maintain a reduced form of the original reinforcement, as opposed to that required to deal with the Tough Kid's initial levels of inappropriate behavior, is in most cases well worth the trouble.

Unique Delivery Systems for Positive Reinforcement

The Wandering Social Reinforcer

One of the most effective, but underused, delivery systems for positive reinforcement is the wandering teacher. The wandering teacher serves several useful purposes. First of all, by wandering **randomly** while students are working independently or in small groups or even while presenting material, the teacher's proximity serves to help **prevent** problems from occurring in the first place. Since random wandering does not allow students to predict when the teacher will be in their location, some inappropriate behavior will simply be avoided altogether.

Wandering provides the teacher with the perfect opportunity to provide positive social reinforcement to students. A smile, wink, nod, or pat on the back can be delivered quickly and easily. Encouragement and quick checks of academic work (with no more than 30 seconds per stop) can serve to keep students who are on-task **on-task** and provide positive corrective feedback where needed.

The teacher who parks at his/her desk and does not circulate is missing many prime opportunities for social reinforcement with students. Additionally, by requiring that students come up to his/her desk for assistance or to have work checked, the teacher is contributing to the escalation of behavior problems. When students

> **"We would recommend that new teachers not be issued desks until they have been teaching for two years!"**

come to the teacher, rather than the teacher to the students, their proximity with each other is increased as they pass desks and wait in line for assistance. Pushing, shoving, and negative comments often result and can blow up into bigger problems.

We would recommend that new teachers not be issued desks until they have been teaching for two years! In this way they would become accustomed to moving around the room and would not establish the bad habit of sitting behind the desk to carry out classroom learning activities.

Chart Moves

Chart Moves make use of a teacher-constructed dot-to-dot picture which is posted so that the student can track his/her own progress, and which determines when the reinforcement will be delivered. Figure 2-2 shows three examples of Chart Moves posters.

With Chart Moves, each time reinforcement is earned, the student is allowed to connect another dot on the chart. He/she then earns the prespecified reward each time the special reward dot is reached. The reward dots are colored or circled to indicate that the student will receive the reinforcement when he/she has earned enough chart moves to reach the special dot. Additionally, the first or last chart move earned each day may be dated, so that a student's daily progress is automatically recorded as the chart is used.

The distance (or number of chart moves) between the special reward dots will vary depend-

ing on the frequency with which the teacher believes the student's behavior needs to be reinforced. It is expected that a student will require fewer chart moves initially to reach the reward dot when he/she is first learning a new behavior. Reward dots are spaced further apart (requiring more chart moves) as the student's behavior improves. Thus, Chart Moves has built into it an effective means of gradually fading the positive reinforcement.

Variations of the use of Chart Moves include making the dot-to-dot chart an actual picture of what the student wishes to earn. For example, a drawing of an ice cream cone, an action figure or a squirt gun might be used as the outline for the chart. Similarly, the student might earn a puzzle piece each time he/she lands on a reward

**Figure 2-2
Chart Moves Examples**

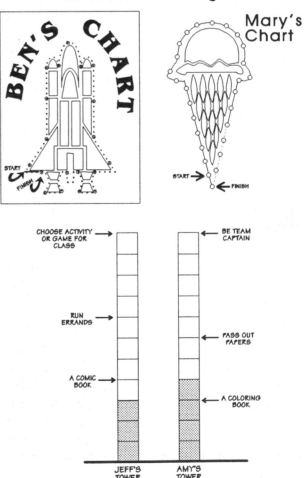

dot. When completed, the puzzle forms a picture of the earned item, and the student receives the item when the puzzle is complete. The student can also earn the privilege of coloring in blocks of a graphed tower. When the student reaches a predetermined level of the tower, certain prespecified positive reinforcement is delivered.

The Chart Moves system is suited for use with many behaviors including noncompliance, throwing tantrums, talk-outs, and peer interactions.

Magic Pens

Another variation of the Chart Moves system is to combine it with the use of magic marker "decoding" pens, available at most office supply stores. (**NOTE:** Pentech International, Inc., markets a set of seven bright watercolor markers plus one liquid eraser pen.) With this strategy, the reward dots are not circled or colored, but rather are marked with an invisible ink magic marker. Each time the student earns a chart move, he/she touches the next dot with the magic decoding pen, which turns the dot a dark color if it has been designated as a reward dot by the invisible ink marker. Thus, reinforcement is unpredictable and will usually result in high performance rates.

Spinners

A game-type "spinner" like the one shown in Figure 2-3 may also be used to reinforce numerous behaviors.

The Spinner is divided into five or more sections of various sizes. Each section of the Spinner represents a different positive reinforcer, such as being first in line to lunch, a new pencil, a drink of water, ten minutes of free time with a friend, or a candy bar for elementary students. Secondary students have been known to enjoy earning coupons exchangeable for gas for their

**Figure 2-3
Spinner Example**

JOHN'S SPINNER

- 15 Minutes Free Time
- Recording on Tape Recorder 30 min. After School
- 10 min. Choice of Game with Friend
- First in Line
- Candy Treat
- 20 Extra Bonus Points
- Surprise Box of Things To Do
- Sit Anywhere in Class
- Get to Pass Out Papers to Class

cars, food from a fast food restaurant, a parking space in front of the school for a day, or hair styling services.

Positive reinforcement represented on the Spinner should be planned and selected with the student so that those positive reinforcers of "higher" value are given a smaller slice of the Spinner. When used in conjunction with the Chart Moves system, the student earns a spin on the Spinner when he/she reaches one of the colored reward dots. Care must be taken to periodically change the positive reinforcement represented on the Spinner so that it retains its original effectiveness.

Mystery Motivators

The first component of the Mystery Motivator is the motivator or reinforcer itself. The name of the reinforcer is written on a slip of paper, sealed inside an envelope, and displayed in a prominent position somewhere in the classroom such as in the middle of the chalkboard at the front of the room. The second component is a monthly chart, on which the teacher has randomly marked reinforcement days with a small colored

"Mystery Motivator"

"X." Each of the days has a self-sticking dot or small piece of masking tape on it. For those days with an "X" on them, the "X" is covered with the dot or tape (see Figure 2-4).

For each day that the student earns reinforcement, he/she is permitted to peel off one dot or piece of tape. If there is an "X" under the dot or tape, the student is given the Mystery Motivator envelope to open. The reinforcement that is named on the piece of paper inside is then delivered. If there is no "X" under the dot or sticker, the student will have to wait until the next day to peel off the next dot. Randomly assigning the "X's" under the dots creates high anticipation and provides a visual reminder each day of what the student must do to earn a chance at the Mystery Motivator.

Magic Pens can also be used effectively with Mystery Motivator charts (see Figure 2-5). With this strategy, the teacher uses the "invisible" pen to mark the days the Mystery Motivator may be earned. Until the student has met the criteria for the day and earned the right to color the box on the chart for that day (revealing the secret "X"), he/she won't know whether a Mystery Motivator will be delivered that day. Of course, if the student fails to meet criteria, he/she will think that that may have been the day the Mystery Motivator would have been delivered.

One critical component to making Mystery Motivators effective is the "hype" associated with presenting them to the class, reminders about the

possibility of earning them, and what may or may not be in the envelope. The teacher must talk about the Mystery Motivators with excitement and anticipation, and make them as **mysterious** as possible. If the teacher does a good job of marketing, Tough Kids will respond enthusiastically. This technique has been used successfully with both elementary and secondary students.

Grab-Bags

Grab-bags are based on essentially the same concept as the Mystery Motivator, except that the reinforcer itself is placed in the bag and is earned when the student uncovers an "X" on his/her randomly marked chart.

The Grab-bag may also be used in conjunction with a Spinner, where the teacher has written "Grab-bag" on one of the Spinner sections. A variation of the Grab-bag is for the bag to contain a number of wrapped items of varying value. When the student has earned the right to the Grab-bag, he/she is allowed to select an item from the bag while not being permitted to view its contents.

Lottery/Raffle Tickets

Passing out Lottery or Raffle Tickets is one way the teacher can reinforce desired academic performance or behavior on a daily basis. How To Box 2-4 outlines guidelines for the use of Lottery or Raffle Tickets.

Students write their names on earned tickets and deposit them in a designated container in the classroom. Depending upon how frequently the teacher needs to reinforce the class, drawings may be held once or twice each day, as well as weekly or monthly for small prizes. The more reinforcement the class requires, the more frequently the teacher will hold the drawings and the more prizes he/she will award each time.

Figure 2-4
Mystery Motivator Chart Samples

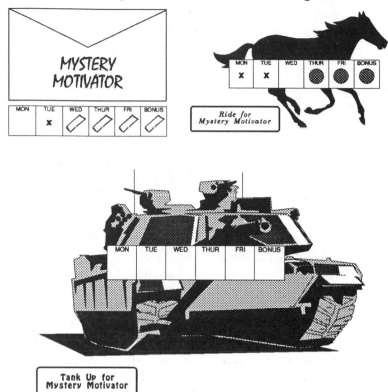

Ride for
Mystery Motivator

Tank Up for
Mystery Motivator

Figure 2-5
Mystery Motivator Chart With Magic Pens

Make Tracks for
Mystery Motivator

Guidelines for Using Lottery/Raffle Tickets

1. Select the specific academic and/or social behaviors you wish to improve.

2. Design or select the tickets.

3. Determine how often initial drawings must be held so that students will be motivated to work for tickets.

4. Explain the program to the students. Tell them the behaviors that will result in their earning the tickets. Give examples of the desired behaviors; role play if necessary to make certain students understand the expectations.

5. Implement the program. Give tickets generously for the targeted behaviors.

6. When giving out each ticket, specifically describe and praise the behavior for which the ticket is being given (e.g., "Alicia, nice job of completing your reading workbook on time.").

7. Be certain to award tickets to students who have not exhibited the targeted behaviors previously, but who are exhibiting them now.

8. Be certain to also award tickets to students who have exhibited the target behaviors in the past and continue to exhibit them. Otherwise, students may get the idea that the only way they will receive reinforcement is if they first fail to behave appropriately.

9. Within two weeks of implementing a daily raffle program or four weeks of implementing a weekly one, evaluate the effectiveness of the program. Make adjustments as needed in the the target behaviors, the prizes which are awarded in the drawings, the frequency of the drawings, and the number of tickets available for students to earn each day.

Prizes in raffle drawings may be small school items such as pencils or other supplies, treats, food coupons, small puzzles, and games and other items donated by local businesses or the PTA. Drawings may also include prizes such as a positive note or phone call home to parents and classroom privileges such as using desirable sports or game equipment at recess, serving as classroom aide for a prespecified time of the day, taking a day off from homework in one subject, and the like.

For weekly (or monthly) drawings, all coupons earned for the week (or month), including those which have already been drawn for prizes, are placed in the container for a drawing. Thus, students know that they still have a chance to win a prize, even if they weren't selected in a daily drawing. For the weekly or monthly drawing, it is suggested that fewer names be drawn and that the prizes be somewhat bigger.

In implementing a daily/weekly/monthly raffle program, the teacher will also need to build in a "cost" or "fine" system so that Tough Kids who have just recently exhibited inappropriate behavior are not rewarded by the system. It is suggested that, to prevent this type of occurrence, a rule be adopted specifying that any student whose inappropriate behavior has necessitated being sent to the office or required a phone call home to parents (or earned another classroom penalty for more severe behavior problems) during that day (for a daily drawing) or during the week before a weekly or monthly drawing be disqualified from collecting a prize if his/her name is drawn in that particular drawing. In order to do this, the teacher will need to keep a list of students who are disqualified should their names be drawn in the raffle. If a disqualified student's name is drawn, it is not necessary to announce the name. The teacher can merely state that the name of someone who is disqualified has been drawn and that another name will be drawn. This procedure maximizes the "fine" system, since all students who have been disqualified for the drawing will think they may have collected a prize had they not been disqualified. Figure 2-6 depicts examples of Raffle Tickets used in different classrooms.

Figure 2-6
Sample Lottery/Raffle Tickets

Summary

It is human nature to react negatively to Tough Kids. If their teachers do what comes naturally, they will be far more negative than positive with these students. Unfortunately, this teacher management style is more than ineffective—it will actually cause an increase in Tough Kids' inappropriate behavior over time!

Positive reinforcement and antecedent strategies must formulate the backbone of any educational program for Tough Kids. While negative consequences can **temporarily** stop or suppress inappropriate behavior, only positive strategies will help build or increase **appropriate** behavior. Thus, it is imperative that at least three or four positives be used with Tough Kids for every negative.

Finding things that Tough Kids consider reinforcing can require a great deal of ingenuity on the part of teachers. However, the effort will pay enormous dividends. Not only will the student benefit from this approach, but the teacher will find his/her classroom a much more positive environment in which to work. An emphasis on the strategies presented in this chapter in combination with the appropriate use of reductive strategies outlined in the following chapter will produce dramatic results!

References

Cautela, J.R. & Brion-Meisels, L. (1979). A children's reinforcement survey schedule. *Psychological Reports, 44,* 327-338.

Clement, P.W. & Richard, R.C. (1976). Identifying reinforcers for children: A children's reinforcement survey. In E.J. Mash & L.G. Terdal (Eds.), *Behavior therapy assessment: Diagnosis, design and evaluation.* New York: Springer.

Dewhurst, D.L. & Cautela, J.R. (1980). A proposed reinforcement survey schedule for special needs children. *Journal of Behavior Therapy and Experimental Psychiatry, 2,* 109-113.

Gelfand, D.M. & Hartmann, D.P. (1984). *Child behavior: Analysis and therapy* (pp. 233-236). New York: Pergamon Press.

Hequet, M. (1990). Non-sales incentive programs inspire service heroes. *Reward and Recognition, 8,* 3-17.

Premack, D. (1959). Toward empirical behavior laws: I. positive reinforcement. *Psychological Review, 66,* 219-233.

Chapter 3

Practical Reductive Techniques for the Classroom

The behaviors that characterize Tough Kids are the behaviors teachers want to stop. These behavioral excesses were detailed in Chapter One, and include aggression, noncompliance, verbal abuse, arguing, tantrum throwing, excuse making, and more. They are the behaviors that drive teachers crazy and make them want to give up teaching. Behavioral excesses literally interfere with learning for both the Tough Kid and other students in the classroom. This chapter focuses on practical classroom procedures that any teacher can use to reduce these problem behaviors. That is why we call these procedures **reductive**.

A word of caution before proceeding. None of the techniques covered in this chapter will change behavior permanently. Teachers cannot implement a reductive technique and expect it to have lasting effects, for two basic reasons. First, these annoying behavioral excesses serve a purpose for Tough Kids. In a sense, they are functional and work for these students. They may help the student avoid tasks, gain attention from peers, or get tangible rewards from the student's environment. If they are to be reduced permanently, these behavioral excesses have to be replaced with appropriate behaviors that also meet the student's needs. Remember our definition of a Tough Kid included both behavioral excesses and deficits. For permanent change, functional abilities in the areas of social skills, academic performance, and self-management skills must **replace behavioral excesses**. These replacement behaviors must work for the Tough Kid as well as the behavioral excesses do.

The second reason that reductive techniques are not permanent behavior change techniques is that Tough Kids are somewhat **immune to punishment**. They build up a resistance to shouts, threats, and even physical abuse, particularly from adults. It has been estimated that Tough Kids can take twice the amount of punishment as regular students and still not

"Immune to Punishment"

change their behavior (Patterson, 1976)! After the second grade through junior high school, the average rate of teacher verbal reprimands in the classroom is once every two minutes (White, 1975; Van Houten & Doleys, 1983). After the second grade, the rate of teacher praise declines rapidly, with the rate of reprimands almost always exceeding praise rates. Tough Kids receive the majority of these reprimands, and they become immune to teachers' yelling, threats, and negative attention.

The only way to make behavior change permanent is to use **positive procedures** to reward appropriate replacement behaviors. Reductive techniques can temporarily reduce the behavioral excesses, but only positive procedures can build the social, academic, and self-management skills that are necessary to replace the excesses.

What Are Reductive Techniques?

For our purposes, a **reductive technique** is any **research-valid** technique that will temporarily stop or suppress a behavior. We prefer to call them reductive techniques, rather than punishment for several reasons. Punishment is loaded with many emotional feelings and is tied to retribution (assumed deserved penalties). The term punishment can also be confusing for teachers.

The practical reductive techniques that are included in this book can be used by teachers to stop behavioral excesses while they work on building appropriate replacement skills. They are all proven effective by research (research-valid). If the teacher uses nonvalid reductive techniques, then he/she will be vulnerable to criticism, personnel action, or legal difficulties if there are problems with the techniques. Only research-valid techniques should be used with Tough Kids.

What specifically are reductive techniques? When we think of reductive techniques, procedures like time out, in-school suspension, names and checks on the board, expulsion, and others come to mind. Some of these procedures are workable with Tough Kids; some are not. The

reductive techniques most frequently used by teachers include verbal reprimand (approximately 42%), parental contact (22%), revokation of privileges (17%), detention (10%), isolation of student from class (6%), principal's office (2%), and corporal punishment (used less than 1% of the time).

Obviously teacher reprimands are the most frequently used reductive technique. The problem with teacher reprimands is that they are overused or not used effectively. These frequently used techniques may not even be the most effective reductive techniques. It is important to use creative reductive techniques that are more positive, such as differential attention, time out (e.g., Bumpy Bunny Time Out), the Compliance Matrix, and the "Sure I Will" program which will be presented later in this chapter. However, to use any of these techniques, it is important to learn the general variables that make them effective.

Effective Use of Reductive Techniques

Learning to use anything effectively means learning to use it with the least amount of "cost" for maximum results. If a technique takes too much time, effort, or classroom resources, then a teacher will not continue to use it. Effective use also means that the technique is used sparingly, not wastefully. If a reductive technique is used too much, it becomes watered down and ineffective. Lastly, teachers want to use this type of technique to produce the largest behavior change possible. To get the most effective results with reductive techniques, five principles msut be followed (see Box 3-1).

Oh No! Not From Someone I Like

Most people dislike having reductive techniques used with them, particularly from someone they like. It is much more difficult to receive a reprimand from a person who truly cares for them, and for whom they care. Almost everyone is familiar with the characterization in movies and on TV of the school disciplinarian whose job is to merely catch and punish students. This person is frequently depicted as pathetic and inept, disliked by students, and often set up and made the brunt of jokes. There is a grain of truth in this characterization.

Box 3-1

Principles That Influence the Effectiveness of Reductive Techniques

Reward rates should be high.

- The rate of reinforcement for appropriate behaviors should be high. It is much more effective for a student to receive a reductive technique from a person he/she likes and finds reinforcing.

Reward an appropriate behavior that interferes with the misbehavior.

- Find a behavior that is incompatible with or an appropriate alternative to the misbehavior to reward so that it can replace the inappropriate behavior.

Do not adapt the student to the reductive technique.

- Do not start off with a less intense form of the reductive technique and slowly work up. Use a form of the reductive technique that is potent enough to result in rapid behavior change so the student does not adapt to it.

Start early in a student's behavior chain of misbehavior.

- Do not wait until the student is out of control. Identify the early "trigger" misbehaviors in a chain (e.g., ignoring, delaying, arguing, etc.) and implement the reductive procedure early.

Manage peer attention to your advantage.

- Use peer attention to reward appropriate behaviors through the use of group contingencies (detailed later in this chapter). Do not allow peers to reward inappropriate behaviors that make the Tough Kid more difficult.

To achieve a **liking effect**, it is important for teachers to reinforce at higher rates than they punish. It has already been pointed out that in all grades after the second grade, teachers' reprimands exceed their rates of praise. This is exactly the effect that is **not** wanted because it causes students to dislike teachers and the classroom in general. A teacher's praise and reinforcement rate must exceed his/her reductive technique rate to be effective. We suggest the simple formula of three or four praise statements (using the IFEED-AV rules from Chapter Two) for every negative statement (e.g., reprimand or criticism) or consequence he/she delivers. Under no circumstances should the teacher give less than four praise statements per hour. More about this later.

You Can't Misbehave and Do That Too—It's Impossible!

This is an excellent technique to make reductive procedures more effective. It simply means that if teachers reinforce an appropriate behavior that actually interferes with the misbehavior, then the misbehavior will be reduced naturally. For example, if a student is a trichotillomanic (constantly pulls or plays with his/her hair) and a teacher rewards the student for keeping his/her hands in his/her pockets (the appropriate behav-

ior), then the hair pulling is naturally reduced. A student cannot pull hair and have his/her hands in his/her pockets at the same time.

This behavior interference principle is simple in theory, but difficult in classroom practice. Teachers must be very creative and think of replacement behaviors that actually interfere with misbehaviors such as arguing, noncompliance, and aggression. The "Sure I Will" program and the Compliance Matrix that are presented later in this chapter are excellent examples of techniques that use the behavior interference principle.

Swimming Pool Effect—Don't Let Them Get Used to the Water

It has already been indicated that most Tough Kids are immune to frequently used reductive techniques such as verbal reprimands. Teachers can make things worse by helping students adapt to reductive techniques even more. Teachers often feel that they must use the least amount of a reductive technique, and then if it is not effective, gradually increase the amount. For instance, a teacher may want to use time out in a chair, beginning with 30 seconds in the chair. The teacher may then increase the time to one minute when the technique fails, then three minutes, then five minutes, then fifteen minutes, then 30 minutes, and so on. In effect, this teacher gradually adapts the student to longer and longer times in the time out chair. It is similar to getting into a swimming pool with cold water. At first you may put only a toe in the water. When it feels warm, you may put more and more of your body in until the water does not feel as cold.

A better way to use reductive techniques is to start with the amount of the technique that the research literature indicates is most effective. For instance, about a minute per year of age of the student is a good guideline for the use of several types of time out. A seven-year old student who behaves very inappropriately should sit in the time out chair for approximately seven minutes. Using too little of a technique and slowly increasing is just as bad as using too much of a reductive technique. Teachers must be familiar enough with each technique to use the correct amount.

Use It Early—Don't Wait For the Explosion

Just like immediate reinforcement, using a reductive technique immediately is critically important, although it may be difficult to judge just how early. Should a teacher wait until the student actually exhibits aggressive behavior, or start earlier? Most Tough Kids' coercive behavior occurs in an escalating chain (see Figure 3-1). The student at first ignores (first link), then delays (second link), then argues (third link), and finally tantrums or is aggressive (fourth link). If teachers wait until the end of the chain to use reductive techniques, they receive the most explosive and difficult behavior. It is much more effective to have a preplanned consequence ready for the first two behavior chain links. This requires that the teacher: (1) does not hold back or wait; (2) anticipates problems by learning to identify the behavior chain links; (3)

has preplanned consequences; and (4) does not try to make "deals," negotiate with, or attempt to placate the Tough Kid once the coercive cycle begins. It will only make the behavior worse.

Peer Attention—Use It to Your Own Advantage

Many of the inappropriate behaviors that Tough Kids exhibit are directly rewarded by peer attention. Since so many Tough Kids have inadequate social skills, they use disruptive classroom behavior to appeal to their peers. Smiles, gestures, dares, and snickers are all subtle reinforcers from peers that encourage Tough Kids to misbehave.

Turning this peer attention to the teacher's advantage is one of the best ways to improve the effectiveness of reductive techniques. However, teachers are often reluctant to use peer attention to improve a Tough Kid's behavior. This does not make sense. If left to chance, peer attention will frequently reward inappropriate Tough Kid behavior and make the situation worse. Later in this chapter using peer attention as a practical tool through peer group contingencies will be detailed.

Figure 3-1
A Behavior Chain

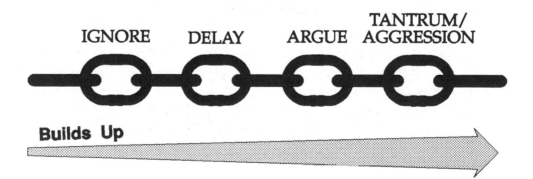

The Reductive Techniques

Request and Reprimand Antecedents—First Line of Defense

As an educator, did anyone ever teach you how to make an effective request or give an effective reprimand? Probably not. Yet teachers are constantly having to ask students to do things in a classroom. Similarly, reprimands, as previously noted, are teachers' most frequently used reductive technique in the classroom.

Request making and reprimands are closely related in several ways. First, most "**Don't**" requests are reprimands. "Don't pull her hair!" "Don't put that in your mouth!" "Don't talk out in my classroom!" are all reprimand forms of requests. Second, all requests or reprimands always precede the behaviors teachers are attempting to stop (such as arguing, noncompliance, tantrums). Because they always come before a behavior, they are called **antecedent** (that which precedes in time). If request and reprimand antecedents are used correctly, teachers will have fewer problems and less noncompliance. If they are used incorrectly, arguing, excuses, tantrums, aggression, and noncompliance will increase. It is easy to use request antecedents correctly. Following are some optimizing variables to remember when making a request or giving a reprimand.

Do Not Use A Question Format

It is a mistake for teachers and parents to phrase a request in a question format. "Isn't it time to get started?" "Wouldn't you like to get your work done?" "Don't you want to please your parents and follow the classroom rules?" All of these are foolish questions. If a teacher can accept "No" for an answer from the student and live with it, then it is reasonable to use a question format. If a teacher cannot live with the "No" answer, then the question format should not be used. "It is time to get started," "Please get your work done," and "I want you to follow the classroom rules because it will please me and your parents" are much better approaches.

Get Up Close

It is interesting to note that many teachers give reprimands at relatively great distances (approximately 15-20 feet) from students. That is why so many teachers end up yelling or making pointing gestures. The greater the distant between a teacher and the student, the more the teacher will yell and make gestures.

Optimally, a request or reprimand should be made at approximately three feet or arms' length. It even improves request efficiency with younger students for the teacher to put his/her hand on students' shoulders as the request is made. If the teacher spends a great deal of time sitting behind his/her desk, it is impossible to take advantage of the optimal distance of three feet. Effective teachers spend as little time as possible behind their desks (see Figure 3-2).

Figure 3-2
Not Too Much Desk Time

They randomly walk around their rooms and actually anticipate problems before they occur.

Use A Quiet Voice

The more teachers yell, the less effective they will be in the classroom. The purpose of yelling is usually to gain a student's attention and increase the emphasis of a request or reprimand. However, a quiet request made close to the student is much more effective than a yelled request from a distance. It also has the added advantage of not disturbing the rest of the class.

Look'em In the Eyes

Eye contact has an important impact in terms of both reinforcement and requests. If teachers look students in the eyes as they make requests, they will get improved compliance. In one study, the teacher requested eye contact, "Look me in the eyes," and then made the request, "Now hang up your coat," or, "Hand in your homework" (Hamlet, Axelrod, & Kuerschner, 1984). She knew it was really working when she got improved compliance overall, and one student walked in the classroom one day and said, "You can stop this 'look at me' stuff. I've all ready hung up my coat and here is my homework"!

Give Them Time

Once a request is made, a student needs a certain amount of time to begin the requested action. About five to ten seconds should be given after a request is made. During this five to ten seconds, the teacher should wait. This **compliance-time window** must not be interrupted. In one study, mothers interrupted during this window 40% of the time by either (1) restating the request unnecessarily, or (2) making an entirely new request before the child had a chance to

comply to the first request (Forehand, 1977). Do not make these mistakes; simply wait. Compliance will be increased by being close to the student in terms of distance, by continuing to make eye contact, and by not talking.

Ask Only Twice—The Nagging Effect

The more times teachers ask, the less compliance they get. Teachers and parents often say, "I have to ask him/her a hundred times before he/she will do anything." This trap is called the nagging effect, and it will greatly reduce compliance. The frequently-asked student has trained adults to ask over and over again. It is not uncommon for teachers to suspect hearing loss in students with good hearing when they use this manipulative strategy.

A teacher should only give a request twice. If the student does not comply, then the teacher must follow through with a preplanned consequence for not complying the first two times when asked. A hierarchy of preplanned consequences and a "What If? Chart" (detailed later in this chapter) are good procedures to use.

Don't Give Multiple Requests

It is easy to string a series of requests together in hope of saving time. However, multiple requests reduce compliance, particularly with Tough Kids. Give one request, wait, follow through, and then issue the next request after the student has complied.

Describe the Request

It is much better to give a detailed request than a global request. Teachers often assume that students know what they want, when they do not understand. For example, saying, "Don't talk out in my class" is less effective than, "You need to raise your hand before you talk in my class." Instructional detail in a request helps focus a student and improve compliance.

Be Nonemotional

The more a teacher gets upset with a Tough Kid, the less compliance the teacher will get. Yelling, threatening gestures, ugly faces, guilt-inducing statements, rough handling, and deprecating comments about the student or his/her family ("I've had problems with your whole family!") only reduce compliance. This type of teacher behavior also destroys the liking principle covered previously.

Make More Start ("Do") Requests Than Stop ("Don't") Requests

Teachers should check themselves. If they make more "Don't" requests, then something is wrong. Possibly their classroom rules are not well-constructed or the other proactive strategies detailed in Chapter One are not being implemented properly. A teacher whose "Don't" requests exceed his/her "Do" requests has a negative classroom. Interestingly, if teachers give too many "Don't" requests, they may actually receive a reduction in compliance to "Do" requests.

Verbally Reinforce Compliance

This seems self-evident, but it is not. First, it is easy for teachers to forget or not notice when students do comply with their requests, and they simply move on to the next task. Second, with some Tough Kids, teachers feel that if they verbally reinforce the students for complying, they will stop the requested behavior (i.e., the "letting sleeping dogs lie" argument). This is completely wrong. If teachers want compliance in the future, they must reward it now.

Box 3-2 summarizes the variables just detailed that affect compliance by students.

"Verbally Reinforce Compliance"

Box 3-2

Variables That Affect Compliance

Do not use a question format when giving a command:

- Do not use such statements as "Isn't it time to do your work?" or "Wouldn't you like to start to work?" Instead make the request a polite command, such as "Please start your work."

Get close to the student when giving a command:

- The optimal distance for giving a command is approximately three feet. Do not give commands from great distances or from behind your desk.

Use a quiet voice, do not yell:

- When giving a command, give it in a quiet voice, up close, with eye contact.

Look students in the eyes:

- Request eye contact when giving a student a command. For example, "John, look me in the eyes. Now I want you to . . . ."

Give the student time:

- When giving a student a command, give him/her from five to ten seconds to respond before (1) giving the command again, or (2) giving a new command.

Do not nag:

- Issue a command only twice, then follow through with a preplanned consequence. The more you request, the less likely you are to gain compliance.

Do not give multiple requests:

- Make only one request at a time. Do not string requests together.

Describe the behavior you want:

- It helps to give specific and well-described requests rather than global requests.

Be nonemotional:

- Be calm, not emotional. Yelling, threatening gestures, ugly faces, guilt-inducing statements, rough handling, and deprecating comments about the student or his/her family only reduce compliance.

Make more start requests than stop requests:

- Requests that start behaviors ("Do" requests) are more desirable than requests that inhibit behaviors ("Don't" requests). The majority of teacher requests should be "Do" requests. If the majority of teacher requests are "Don't" requests, it probably means the classroom rules or planned consequences are poorly designed or are not being implemented correctly.

Verbally reinforce compliance:

- It is easy to forget and not socially reward a student when he/she complies to your request. If you do not reward the student, compliance will decrease.

Precision Requests

It helps in dealing with a Tough Kid if all of the classroom staff use the same procedures. The big problem in getting Tough Kids to stop their arguing and noncompliance is that each staff member has a different approach to making requests. Some staff talk too much as they try to reason a student into compliance. Other staff threaten, use guilt, or yell at the student. It is better to synchronize request-making behavior for all classroom staff to achieve maximum compliance.

A precision request takes all the compliance variables listed above and combines them into a standard approach (see Figure 3-3).

The following are steps to use precision requests effectively:

Step 1   The teacher explains the precision request and its consequences to the whole class before the procedure is started.

Step 2   A quiet "Please" request (such as, "Please get your materials out and start working.") is made in a nonquestion format, up close, with eye contact.

Step 3   The teacher waits 5-10 seconds after making the request and does not interact with the student during this time.

Step 4   If the student starts to comply, he/she is verbally reinforced using the IFEED-AV rules (refer to Chapter Two).

Step 5   If the student does not comply within five to ten seconds, a second request is given with the signal word "need" (such as, "Now I **need** you to get your materials out and start working.").

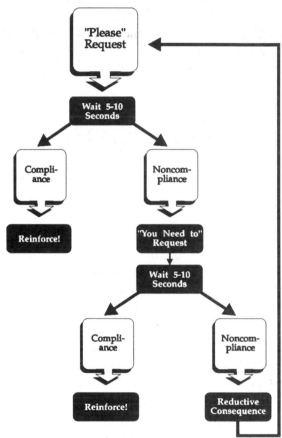

Figure 3-3
Precision Request Sequence

Step 6   If the student starts to comply, he/she is verbally reinforced using the IFEED-AV rules.

Step 7   If the student still does not comply within five to ten seconds, the teacher implements a preplanned reductive consequence.

Step 8   After the reductive consequence, the teacher again repeats the request using the signal word "need." If the student complies, he/she is reinforced. If not, the next preplanned consequence from the hierarchy is used.

There are several important components to a precision request. First, the signal word "need" is important because it signals the message, "You have only one more chance before I implement a reductive consequence." Second, it is essential that once a student has experienced the reductive consequence, the teacher immediately repeats the request. If the request is not repeated, Tough Kids can escape the original request simply by receiving a consequence. The message must be that even if the student receives a reductive consequence, he/she will still be required to comply with the original request.

Frequently teachers ask, "What happens if the student still will not comply after he/she has experienced a consequence?" The answer is that a hierarchy of consequences must be preplanned and implemented. If one consequence does not work, then a teacher should move on to the next. The trick is designing a hierarchy which includes effective practical reductive consequences.

Designing a Hierarchy of Consequences

The worst time to select a reductive consequence is in the midst of the arguing, tantrum throwing, and yelling involved in a coercive episode. When a consequence is selected at that time, the temptation is to use an ultimate consequence ("Nuke'em") because the teacher is upset. In this case, delivering a harsh consequence may feel good. An **ultimate** consequence is one that is too severe for the behavior. Teachers know that a consequence is an ultimate consequence as soon as the words leave their mouths; they know it is overly harsh or impossible to follow through. Most ultimate consequences are poorly designed, unrealistic consequences that have open-ended time limits, are based on someone feeling good (generally the teacher) before they are stopped, or have unreasonable expectations. Examples of consequences which are too severe for the misbehavior (ultimate consequences) are statements such as:

- "You are out of my room for good; nobody does that in my classroom," or "I absolutely will not have him back in my classroom." (open-ended time limit)
- "You have lost your recess privileges (or other privilege) for being irresponsible. I will tell you when I think you are ready to get them back." (an open-ended time limit and someone must feel good—the teacher)
- "Get down to the principal's office; you'll have to stay there until I say you can come back." (someone must feel good–the teacher)
- "You are expelled, and you can't come back until your parent(s) come in and guarantee you will behave." (unreasonable expectations—too harsh and unrealistic)

"You are expelled!"

- "Give me all of your books and materials. If you play with things, then you can't have anything—just sit until you can behave." (open-ended time limit)

A much better and safer approach to applying reductive consequences is a preplanned **What If? Chart** (see Figure 3-4). This chart lists reductive consequences (on the right side), along with how much or how long each consequence will be used. The reductive consequences increase in severity as they go down the hierarchy on the chart (see Box 3-3 for examples of reductive consequences).

The reductive consequences are used **only** if: (1) preestablished classroom rules are broken (see Chapter One), or (2) if a student does not comply with a precision request. If a misbehavior occurs that is not addressed in the rules, then the classroom rules should be reexamined. Most well-designed classroom rules will evolve and be

Figure 3-4
What If? Chart

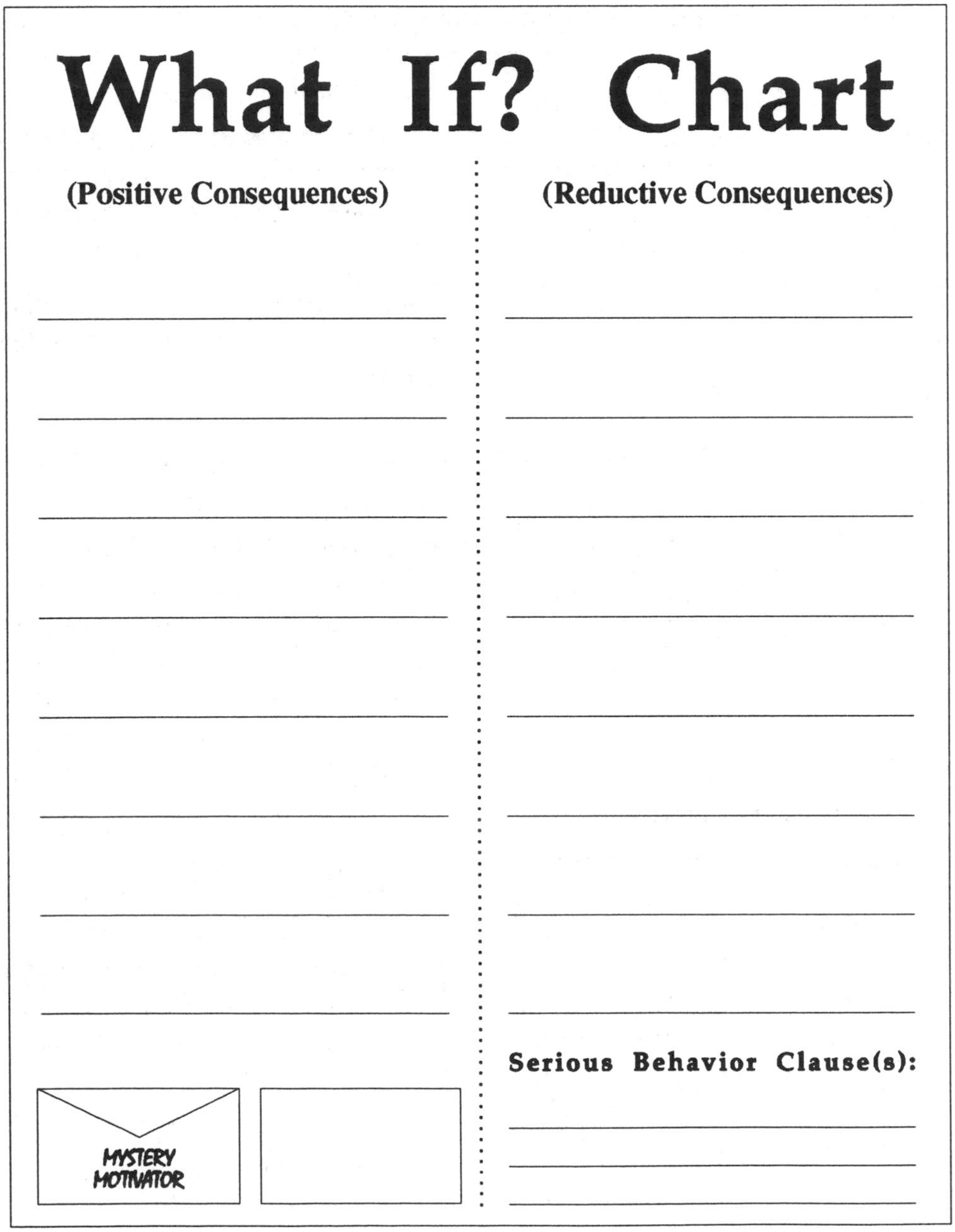

What If? Chart

(Positive Consequences) | **(Reductive Consequences)**

MYSTERY MOTIVATOR

Serious Behavior Clause(s):

Box 3-3

Reductive Consequence Examples for the What If? Chart*

- Verbal warning from the teacher

- Teacher writes student's name down in the Consequence Book

- Student required to wait three minutes in his/her seat when the class is dismissed

- Loss of five minutes of recess or free time (student must sit at his/her desk and work or wait)

- Loss of ten minutes of recess or free time (student must sit at his/her desk and work or wait)

- Extra practice math or spelling assignment for all of recess or free time

- Loss of rewarding activity (e.g., computer time, art activity)

- Required to eat lunch in the classroom

- Not allowed to use the school vending machines

- Must sit in the desk near the teacher for the day

- Student must call his/her parent at home or work in the presence of the teacher and explain the problem behavior and what he/she will do to improve

- Student must walk to the principal's office with the teacher and explain the problem behavior to the principal and what he/she will do to improve

*These consequences are not listed in hierarchy form. The teacher must decide on the hierarchy from least to most reductive.

---

refined over time; they should handle the most difficult behaviors exhibited in a classroom.

In addition to less serious classroom misbehaviors, extreme or dangerous misbehaviors can occur. A **What If? Chart** hierarchy must include a preplanned set of consequences (serious behavior clauses) for crisis or out-of-control behaviors, as these misbehaviors can be dangerous as well as greatly disrupt the classroom. Crisis misbehaviors include blatant or defiant noncompliance, a continuing physical fight, carrying a weapon, physical destruction of property (such as fire setting), or long-duration tantrums that include yelling, swearing, or screaming. These behaviors are rare, but their crisis nature requires preplanned consequences that may temporarily remove the student from the classroom (see Box 3-4 for examples).

You may need extra help to implement the serious behavior clause. A two-way school intercom can be used to summon help, or another student can be sent to the principal's office or another teacher's classroom. The steps to request help should be predesigned in a faculty meeting by the faculty and principal before they are implemented.

All too often only negative reductive consequences are listed on classroom **What If? Chart** hierarchies. The chart in Figure 3-4 also lists positive consequences that students will receive if they follow the classroom rules on the left side. This approach offers a well-balanced approach to classroom consequences. Box 3-5 lists several positive consequences that can be used with the whole class for following classroom rules.

Box 3-4

Serious Behavior Clause Examples for the What If? Chart

- Student must go to another classroom for 20 minutes (i.e., Interclass Time Out)

- Student will be escorted to the principal's office and must sit there for 30 minutes, apologize, and formulate a plan to improve his/her behavior in order to reenter class

- In-school suspension (see How To Box 3-4 on in-school suspension)

- Student's parent will be called at home or work to talk with him/her on the telephone about the behavior, or his/her parent will be required to come to school

- Student will be suspended to home for one day for assault, possession of a weapon, or substantial property destruction; additionally, the police will be called

In addition, the **What If? Chart** has a Mystery Motivator (see Chapter Two) envelope at the bottom as an ultimate reward for the class. The Mystery Motivator can be given randomly once or twice a week to students who have not moved below the first level on the reductive half of the **What If? Chart**, or it can be given to the student who has improved the most or tried the hardest on an academic assignment.

The box to the right of the Mystery Motivator is for teachers to publicly post for themselves the number of positive comments they plan to make to the class. A minimum of three or four positive comments for every negative comment or consequence is recommended. This means that if frequent negative comments or consequences are necessary, the number of positive comments will need to increase accordingly to maintain this ratio. Even if negative comments or conse-

quences are infrequent, a minimum of four positive comments per classroom contact hour for each teacher, aide, or volunteer is suggested. Thus, if teaching is conducted for six hours, then 24 positive comments per day by each member of the teaching staff is the minimum (6 hours X 4 comments = 24). This is not 24 positive comments per student, but 24 to the whole class by each staff member. The number 24 is written in the box with a water-based marker to remind and challenge the teaching staff. It's also a good idea for staff to keep a private tally of their own positive comments, particularly staff who tend to be critical. It is the option of the teaching staff to tell the class what the number 24 means. However, it works well to keep the number a staff secret and to vary the number daily (e.g., 24, 27, 30, 25, etc.).

Box 3-5

Positive Consequence Examples (for the Whole Class) for the What If? Chart

- Names of student superstars will be written on the blackboard (i.e., students can come up to board and write their own names). (This list can include the whole class throughout the day.)

- A note will be sent home for three randomly selected students explaining what a **good** job they have done

- The teacher will read for an extra ten minutes from a high interest adventure book

- Students will be selected to walk to the principal's office and sign their names in the Class Superstars Book. This book will be shown to parents during parent-teacher conferences. (It helps if the Tough Kid is sometimes selected for this reward.)

- Extra free time or a special activity for the whole class

- Randomly selected students are allowed to work at the teacher's desk

- Extra snack for whole class (e.g., popcorn party)

- One homework assignment is dropped for the day

- The whole class is allowed to eat lunch in a special place (e.g., on the school lawn, in a park, or in class while watching a video)

- The class is allowed to view ten minutes of a high interest videotape (i.e., if the teacher has an in-class videotape player, a movie can also be used)

- The class is allowed an extra ten minutes of game time (e.g., compliance games—see How To Box 3-6 on behavioral momentum)

- The teacher will videotape the class working, and play it back to students at the break

- Students are allowed to sit where they want in the classroom for the day

- A student is allowed to select a class-wide reinforcer from a reinforcement menu (see Chapter Two)

- A student is allowed to spin a reinforcement spinner for a class reward (see Chapter Two)

Peer Influence: How to Use It Advantageously

"Look at me-e-e-e-e-e-e!"

A great many misbehaviors exhibited by Tough Kids are for the benefit of their peers. Since Tough Kids are often lacking in social skills, they frequently seek peer attention by misbehaving and disrupting the classroom. Encouragement is often given by peers in the form of smiles, comments, snickers, or subtle gestures. It is clearly to the teacher's advantage to turn this around and manage peer attention to encourage appropriate behavior. The most effective means to do this is through the use of group contingencies that apply rewards and reductive consequences to the class as a whole.

Is it fair to give or take privileges away from the classroom as a group? It is fair if there is evidence that peers are encouraging the misbehavior of Tough Kids. Teachers should look around their classrooms. Is there a group of students that fuel their Tough Kids' behavior problems? If teachers want to facilitate cooperation through peer attention for appropriate behavior, then a group contingency can be a powerful approach.

Designing appropriate group contingencies is critical. First, **never** use a group contingency if a student is learning a new behavior or skill but does not yet have it mastered. Use group contingencies only for behaviors that a student **can** perform, but chooses **not** to perform (e.g., follow classroom rules, hand in homework, pay attention in class). Second, make sure that the criterion is both explained well to students and is attainable. Third, publicly post feedback on

how close students are to either gaining a reward or losing a privilege. Fourth, it is generally **not** good practice to single out one student to perform the behavior criterion. It is better to collect behavior criteria from the classroom as a whole (e.g., total number of talk-outs each day). Or, collect behavior criteria from one or more randomly selected students and evaluate their behavior or performance privately (e.g., select three students randomly, determine if they returned their homework, and grade it to determine if it is at least 80% complete and 80% correct). When selecting random students, it may not be necessary for the class to know exactly who was evaluated. The teacher needs only to inform the class that three students were picked and what the average percentage of the performance (returned homework, on-task rates, number of talk-outs, tardies) was.

One caution. Sometimes Tough Kids will intentionally sabotage group contingencies to ruin the chances for their peers to gain a reward. These Tough Kids thrive on negative peer attention. When this negative pattern occurs, the student should be made a group all by himself/herself. The Tough Kid should lose the privilege of participating with the class until he/she indicates and by appropriate behavior demonstrates that he/she will not intentionally engage in sabotage.

Group contingencies can be used with a variety of consequences. They are particularly effective with the more potent reductive consequences or with positive classroom systems such as the "Sure I Will" program or the Compliance Matrix that will be detailed later in this chapter.

The basic steps for implementing a group contingency are listed in How To Box 3-1, with cautions.

How To Box 3-1

Implementing a Group Contingency

1. Is a group contingency really necessary?

   a. Do peers contribute to the Tough Kid's misbehavior through encouragement or subtle behaviors?

   b. Is improved student cooperation necessary for this behavior?

   c. Have other positive approaches failed to change this behavior?

2. Define the target behavior. Is it observable, measurable, and easily tracked?

3. Is the student capable of the target behavior, but unwilling to perform it?

   a. Make certain the student is not in the process of learning the behavior.

   b. Make certain the student can perform the behavior.

4. Define the group contingency criterion:

   a. Will the criterion be based on the total number of behaviors (e.g., total number of talk-outs)?

   b. Will the criterion be based on the average of the classroom (e.g., 80% of homework returned by the class)?

   c. Will the criterion be based on the performance of one student (e.g., if any student goes to time out)? **Caution**—because of the severity of this criterion, it is generally not advised.

   d. Will the criterion be based on an average of a set number of randomly selected students (e.g., Three students will be selected at random and not identified; if they have handed in their homework and the work is 80% complete and 80% correct, then the class will be rewarded.)?

5. Describe to the class the positive reinforcers that can be gained by the group. Ask for the group's input (e.g., class is permitted to select a reward from the reinforcer menu).

6. Describe to the class a mild reductive consequence if the criterion is not met (e.g., class loses free time period). **Caution**—Make sure the reductive consequence is not overly harsh or for too long a period (e.g., loss of privilege for a week is too long). The loss should be for a day or less.

7. Post the rules for the group contingency. These rules might include:

   a. No threats or making fun of a student who has difficulty will be allowed.

   b. Students may encourage others to do their best.

8. Publicly post the following group contingency information:

   a. The criterion for gaining a reward or losing a privilege— specific target behavior defined with the actual performance number (e.g., no more than five classroom talk-outs);

   b. How the students are doing (e.g., marks on the board for the number of talk-outs); and

   c. What the students will win or lose.

9. Plan a back up procedure for a student who sabotages the group contingency—make the student a team by himself/herself.

10. Make certain that the group contingency plan is **written**, and that:

   a. All classroom staff understand the program;

   b. All the students understand the program;

   c. The program is discussed with the school principal and has his/her support; and

   d. Parents are informed.

11. Emphasize the positive and cooperative aspect of the group contingency.

Potent Reductive Consequences

Up to this point, most of the reductive conse- quences suggested for a **What If? Chart** have been designed for general use in the classroom. In addition to these general consequences, more potent reductive consequences may be needed for Tough Kids. This section will detail three additional consequences: the Response Cost Lottery, time out, and in-school suspension.

Response Cost Lottery

A response cost is simply a "fine" system or losing something one has. Library fines, speed- ing tickets, or late penalties on loans are all examples of common everyday response costs. The problem with most response cost ap- proaches used in classrooms is that teachers can take away most privileges only once, and then they are gone. For example, students can lose their recess or free time only a limited number of times in a day.

The Response Cost Lottery is a technique that research has shown to be especially effective with Tough Kids (Witt & Elliot, 1982; Proctor & Morgan, 1991). One advantage of this tech- nique is that the number of times it can be used with a Tough Kid is not nearly as limited as that of many other techniques.

Figure 3-5
Team Envelope With Tickets for the
Response Cost Lottery

For a Response Cost Lottery, a teacher fills an envelope with five or more tickets for each student, with the student's name written on each

"Did I win?"

ticket. An envelope is taped to each student's desk. If a student breaks a rule or does not follow the teacher's request, then a ticket is removed from that student's envelope. At the end of the day the teacher collects all the tickets remaining in each student's envelope and puts them in a grab-bag. The tickets are then mixed up, and three or four student names are drawn out as in a lottery. The students whose names are drawn receive a reward (e.g., Mystery Motivator or choice of a reward from a reinforcer menu). Students quickly learn that the more tickets they have left in their envelopes, the more likely they are to win the lottery.

To enhance the effects of the Response Cost Lottery, it can easily be combined with a group contingency. For example, teams can be formed (e.g., all students in a row of desks, half the class on each team, or all students sitting at a table). Only one envelope is taped on one desk for each team (see Figure 3-5). When any team member misbehaves, a ticket is withdrawn from the team envelope, thus reducing the overall chances for the whole team of winning the lottery. If group contingencies are used with the Response Cost Lottery, it is important to make sure that the teams are balanced and not all the Tough Kids are on one team, or the procedure could backfire.

A **wild card** ticket can also be used with the group contingency Response Cost Lottery. A wild card is simply one ticket that is always in the grab-bag. If it is drawn, then any team that has a ticket in the grab bag receives the reward. The wild card ticket works to keep teams with low numbers of tickets still motivated and working. If they lose their last ticket in their envelope, then they have no chance of winning the lottery. However, if they have even one ticket there is a chance they can still win with the wild card.

Time Out

Many teachers shy away from using time out because they feel they need a time out room and a set of complicated procedures. Time out is not a place, rather it is a procedure whereby **a student is removed from a reinforcing environment to a less reinforcing environment when misbehavior occurs**. If a teacher complains that a student would rather be in time out instead of the classroom, then the reinforcement rate may be too low in the classroom. Teachers cannot assign a time out from a nonreinforcing environment (it is impossible). The problem is that many classes are nonreinforcing environments, so time out will not work.

A student can often remain in the classroom when time out is used (nonseclusionary time out). For instance, **Bumpy Bunny Time Out** is an in-class time out procedure (see How To Box 3-2).

If a student is reinforced by work materials but continues to misbehave, then the materials can simply be removed and the student ignored (by the teacher and other students) for a short period of time. Similarly, a student may be removed to a time out chair for **Sit and Watch Time Out**. With Sit and Watch Time Out, the student is

allowed to observe the classroom but not participate. If observing makes the misbehavior worse, then the chair can be turned to a wall or corner (**Nonobservation Time Out**). Both of these time out procedures are useful for students who are only mildly disruptive. If a student continues to misbehave or get out of the chair, then more potent forms of time out may be necessary. Do not discount in-class time out procedures without trying them first.

More potent forms of time out require that a student leave the classroom. **Interclass Time Out** is an excellent procedure for more difficult students. This procedure requires that a student be removed to another classroom to work on an academic assignment for a limited period of time (generally 20 to 30 minutes). It is important, if possible, to pick a class one or two grade levels **above** the student's current grade level (e.g., a third grader would go to a fifth grade classroom). This ensures that the Tough Kid will not have same age peers in the time out classroom, and is also effective because students do not want to go into classrooms with older students. If this is not possible, pick a classroom one or two grade levels below the

How To Box 3-2

Procedures for Implementing a Bumpy Bunny Time Out

Bumpy Bunny Time Out is a time out procedure that can be used with younger students (i.e., preschool through the fourth grade). It is called Bumpy Bunny Time Out because it is based on the desires of a little boy who wanted to take his toy bunny (Bumpy) to school to show his friends. However, a student's choice of any desired toy will do. Implementation of Bumpy Bunny Time Out is as follows:

1. Make a space in the classroom in which toys can be displayed while students are working. For example, the top of a bookshelf is perfect.

2. Tape off the last three feet of the bookshelf with red tape. Do not put toys in this area.

3. Invite the students to bring a toy of their choice to the classroom to play with before class or during free time, breaks, or recess.

4. The rules of toy selection and play are:

   a. Toys are brought to class on Monday. If a student does not bring a toy on Monday, he/she has to select a toy from the classroom box (supplied by the teacher) for the week.

   b. Only one toy can be brought to class each week. The same toy is used for the whole week. After a week's time, a new toy can be brought into the classroom and the old toy returned home.

   c. No toy weapons can be selected.

   d. Toys cannot be exchanged, sold, or loaned. If a student violates this rule, he/she loses the toy privilege for one week.

   e. Fights over toys result in a loss of toy privileges for the next day.

   f. All toys are put away (but visible on the bookshelf) during classroom work times.

5. If a student misbehaves or does not follow a teacher's request (precision request), his/her toy is placed in the time out area (the red taped bookshelf area) for three to five minutes (see Figure 3-6) during the next toy playing period (i.e., recess, break). During this time, the student must wait at his/her desk while the other students are allowed to play. For multiple occurrences of noncompliance, the time can accumulate for toy time out (e.g., three "No"s to teacher requests adds up to nine minutes of toy time out).

6. After the time out period the student is allowed to join the other students with his/her toy and play.

student (but resist the temptation to say, "If you act immature, then you have to go to the younger students' classroom."). It is also essential that this procedure be preplanned with the teacher in the time out classroom, and that an academic assignment is ready and waiting for the student.

In order to return to the student's own classroom, it is expected that the assigned work will have been completed.

Figure 3-6
Bumpy Bunny Time Out

Seclusionary Time Out

Seclusionary Time Out is the most severe form of time out procedure to be used with a Tough Kid. With this procedure, a student is removed from the classroom and placed in a special time out room. The room **must** be a room with no other purpose than to be used as a time out room. It should be nonthreatening, clean, well lighted, and well ventilated. It must also have an observation window or device. A student must never be left unattended by a staff member in the room. Thus, unless a staff member is available to supervise a student in the time out room, this form of time out is not an option. How To Box 3-3 lists a series of procedures that should be used with Seclusionary Time Out.

Several steps can be taken to enhance the effectiveness of time out procedures. First, make sure the reinforcement rate in the classroom is sufficiently high. Remember, students cannot be given time out from a nonreinforcing classroom; it is impossible. Second, combine time out with a precision request sequence. This sequence will improve the overall effectiveness of time out. Third, when a student finishes time out, restate the original request ("Now I need you to . . ."). Do not allow a student to escape the request simply by experiencing time out.

Fourth, use a reasonable amount of time for each time out episode. A minute or less per year of age of the student is a good guideline for most elementary students. For instance, if the student is seven years old, then seven minutes or less is an appropriate time out period. Sometimes, less amounts of time can be used effectively; however, do not get caught in the "swimming pool effect" trap of slowly increasing the time out duration. An exception to this guideline is with the use of Interclass Time Out. Generally, a minimum of 20 to 30 minutes in the other classroom is required.

Fifth, reinforce Tough Kids for not needing time out. If a student is having difficulty with four time outs per day, set a daily limit of two time outs. If the student can manage to keep his/her time outs to two or less per day, then the student can earn a privilege or small reward.

How To Box 3-3

Seclusionary Time Out Procedures

1. Seclusionary Time Out should not be used unless all other procedures have been tried and failed. This should be a last effort technique.

2. Seclusionary Time Out should never be used without a parent's written consent.

3. Seclusionary Time Out should be used only if it is listed as an approved and agreed upon technique in a student's Individualized Education Plan (IEP) by the IEP Team. The student should only be placed in time out for approved behaviors on the IEP such as aggression, severe noncompliance, or destructive tantrum throwing.

4. Seclusionary Time Out is defined as removing a student from a reinforcing classroom setting to a less reinforcing setting. This setting can be another classroom, a chair or desk outside of the classroom, or a room specifically approved for time out. If a room is used for time out, it should be used only for time out and no other purpose (e.g., storage, counseling students, or a special academic work area).

5. The time out setting should be well lighted, well ventilated, nonthreatening, and clean. It must also have an observation window or device. The staff member should try the technique on himself/herself before using the room with a student, and the room should be shown to the student's parent(s).

6. The entire time out procedure should be explained to the student before it is implemented, prior to the occurrence of misbehavior which will result in its use.

7. If misbehavior occurs, identify it. For example, tell the student in a calm, neutral manner, "That's fighting; you need to go to the time out room." Tell the student to remove his/her jewelry, belt, and shoes. Tell the student to empty his/her pockets (in order to check for such items as pens, pencils, paper clips, knives, etc.). The student's socks should be checked for these types of items also. If the student does not comply with these requests, call for help and then remove the items and check the pockets yourself. **No other conversation should ensue.**

8. When a student is placed in the time out room, he/she must be constantly monitored by a staff member. The student must never be left alone.

9. When a student is placed in the time out room, the following information should be placed in a **time out log**:

    a. name of the student;

    b. date;

    c. staff member responsible for monitoring student;

    d. time in and time out; and

    e. target behavior warranting the procedure.

10. The student should be placed in the time out room for a specific period of time. A recommended formula is one minute per year of age (e.g., 10-year old student X 1 minute = 10 minutes).

11. If a student is screaming, throwing a tantrum, or yelling, he/she should be quiet (i.e., quiet for 30 consecutive seconds) before being released from the time out room. This 30 seconds does not begin until the one minute per year of age time period has elapsed.

12. Communication between the supervising staff member and the student should not take place when the student is in the time out room (i.e., do not talk with the student, threaten the student, or try to counsel the student at this time).

13. Do remain calm while taking a student to the time out room. Do not argue with, threaten, or verbally reprimand the student.

14. If a student refuses to go to the time out room, add on time to the specified time out duration (e.g., one minute for each refusal, up to five minutes).

15. If a student refuses to come out of the time out room, do not beg or try to remove the student. Simply wait outside, and sooner or later the student will come out on his/her own.

16. If the student makes a mess in the time out room, require him/her to clean it up before he/she leaves.

17. Once the time out period has ended, return the student to the ongoing classroom activity, making sure the student is required to complete the task he/she was engaged in prior to the time out period. This will ensure that students do not purposely avoid unpleasant tasks by going to the time out room.

18. All staff members should be trained, and this training documented before time out procedures are started.

19. To ensure the effectiveness of time out, the reinforcement rate for appropriate behaviors in the classroom should meet the recommended rate of three or four positives to each negative (and never below four positives per contact hour).

How To Box 3-3 cont'd

20. Data should be collected on target behaviors. If time out is effective, these behaviors should decrease shortly after the technique is started. If they do not, check that the procedure is being used correctly and the reinforcement rate for appropriate behavior in the classroom is high enough; and consider another technique for possible use.

21. The use of time out should not be threatened ("If you do that again, I will put you in the time out room.").

Rather, the technique should be combined with a precision request, such as, "I need you to stop ...." If the student persists, the time out procedure should be used, and when the student comes out of the time out room the precision request should be restated ("I need you to ... ").

22. The student should be reinforced for not needing time out.

In-School Suspension

The use of in-school suspension is a form of extended time out to a preselected setting within the school. In-school suspension is a reasonable alternative to more extreme consequences (that can make things worse), such as suspension or expulsion from the school. In-school suspension is generally reserved for very difficult behavior such as fighting, teacher defiance, destruction of property, or repeated truancy. The use of in-school suspension requires a special physical location to detain students, monitoring by a staff member, and assigned academic work. Frequently, in-school suspension can be used for relatively short periods of time, such as two hours to half a day. More extended periods of one or more days are generally not needed. How To Box 3-4 lists the basic guidelines for setting up an effective in-school suspension program.

How To Box 3-4

In-School Suspension Procedures

In-school suspension is an alternative to out of school suspension (being sent home). It should be reserved for very difficult target behaviors (e.g., fighting, teacher defiance, arguing, property destruction, and repeated truancy or tardiness).

1. Decide on a physical place for in-school suspension (e.g., another classroom, desk space in an office, or a carrel).

2. In-school suspension should always occur under the direct observation of a staff member. If students cannot be constantly supervised, in-school suspension should not be used.

3. Time lengths for in-school suspension will usually not exceed several hours to a day. In-school suspension lengths of more than one day are not advisable.

4. When students warrant in-school suspension they should be placed in it immediately. No waiting lists should exist for in-school suspension.

5. In school suspension should have rules, including:

   a. no talking to other students;

   b. no sleeping;

How To Box 3-4 cont'd

c.   stay in your seat; and

d.   work on your school assignments.

6. Students should be given academic assignments to work on during in-school suspension. This work can be actual classroom work or extra assigned work.

7. If a student refuses to go to in-school suspension or shows up late, the time period can be expanded. For example, a student who refuses to go to in-school suspension should have his/her time increased from two hours to half a day, to three quarters of a day, or to a full day. If the student still refuses, the student's parent(s) should be called.

8. Before in-school suspension is started, the student's parent(s) should be informed and consent given whenever possible.

Positive Reductive Techniques

Positive reductive procedures for reducing inappropriate behavior may seem like a contradiction. However, several innovative techniques exist that actually reward the **nonoccurrence** of misbehavior or actually interfere with misbehavior. The more potent reductive techniques may be needed initially with Tough Kids. However, positive reductive techniques are especially useful in maintaining the positive balance in classrooms that serve Tough Kids.

Differential Attention

Many teachers naturally use differential attention and don't even know it. Or, they may know this technique as "accentuate the positive—ignore the negative" or "proximity praise." By whatever name, differential attention is an effective technique that helps reduce both common misbehaviors and the rate of teacher reprimands. The technique is called **differential attention** because the teacher differentially (separately) pays attention to appropriate behavior and ignores inappropriate behavior.

Differential attention combines two basic strategies. First, when a misbehavior occurs the teacher **ignores it**. Ignoring is a difficult technique for teachers because it requires them to do nothing when an irritating behavior is occurring. Doing nothing is difficult, particularly when students are misbehaving in order to get their attention. Ignoring is also difficult because the misbehavior will usually get worse before it gets better. This predictable increase is called an **extinction burst** and is a sign that the technique is working. To ignore, it helps if a teacher breaks eye contact, does not speak to the student, walks away, or engages in another behavior (e.g., reading, talking with another student, writing something, etc.). A mother in one of the author's parent training groups found the perfect ignoring activity to be vacuuming. She said it was a perfect ignoring activity because the machine made a lot of noise and drowned out the arguing, she broke eye contact with the child while she concentrated on the activity, and vacuuming made her move constantly.

"This mom has the ignoring technique down pat!"

The second component of differential attention is to find something the student is doing appropriately and to praise the behavior. It helps to use the IFEED-AV reward rules covered in Chapter Two, especially "D," describing the appropriate behavior. This might mean having to wait for an appropriate behavior or even praising the smallest behavioral improvement.

Sometimes teachers complain that a student never does anything appropriately. However, there is always something to praise. Facetiously: "Good breathing! I love the way you get air into your lungs"; or "Great taking up space! You fill volume better than any one in this classroom." If a student is alive and breathes or takes up space, the student can be praised. The teacher must be creative and find the smallest behaviors to praise. They are always there (e.g., "I appreciate the way you are sitting," "Nice paying attention," or "Now that's the way to get to work.")

One way to use differential attention is to ignore the misbehavior of a student, wait, and then praise his/her appropriate behavior. A second approach is to ignore the student who is misbehaving and praise a student seated nearby for his/her appropriate behavior (**proximity praise**). How To Box 3-5 gives the steps for both of these types of differential attention.

Some words of caution are required for differential attention. It is important to realize that most misbehaviors will temporarily get worse before they get better (extinction burst) when they are ignored. Differential attention works best for behaviors that require the teacher's attention and thus make the teacher's ignoring effective (i.e., complaining, whining, clowning, etc.). It is less effective for aggression or noncompliance when the student hopes the teacher will not notice him/her. Teachers should also realize that if the ignored behavior gets out of hand, they may need to use a precision request followed by a more potent reductive consequence ("Now I need you to stop arguing," followed by a consequence).

The beauty of differential attention is that it reduces the number of unnecessary teacher reprimands. Instead of a continuous stream of "Don't" reprimands, differential attention can be used. It helps if a teacher routinely tries a differential attention approach before giving a "Don't" reprimand or a precision request for minor, attention-getting behaviors.

Behavioral Momentum

Has a salesman ever tried to sell you encyclopedias? If he asked you directly to buy $900.00 worth of books, you would probably refuse. Instead he uses a momentum strategy such as:

- "Do you value truth and knowledge?" ("Yes.");

- "Do you cherish books?" ("Yes.");

- "Would you want your family exposed to truth and knowledge through books?" ("Yes.");

- Then he asks if you would like to buy the encyclopedias.

The salesman has used questions to increase your positive agreement momentum by saying "Yes." Momentum is easily visualized if you imagine a large round rock on the slope of a hill.

How To Box 3-5

Implementing Differential Attention

1. Is the behavior dependent upon the teacher's attention (i.e., whining, complaining, clowning, etc.)? If so, differential attention will probably work. If the behavior does not require the teacher's attention (i.e., noncompliance, aggression, etc.), then differential attention may not work.

2. The teacher should ignore the inappropriate behavior by not paying attention to it, walking away, breaking eye contact, not saying anything to the student, or busying himself/herself with another activity (e.g., reading).

3. When the student stops the inappropriate behavior, the teacher should wait a few moments, and then catch the student being good. He/she should describe and praise the appropriate behavior (e.g., "Bubba—great working on your math assignment."). Teachers can use the IFEED-AV rules for social reinforcement described in Chapter Two.

4. When the teacher ignores, he/she should be prepared for an "extinction burst"; it is temporary, but the behavior is likely to get worse before it gets better. **Caution**–If the teacher breaks down during an extinction burst and pays attention to the student, the teacher is teaching the student that if he/she misbehaves to an even greater extent the misbehavior will be rewarded.

5. The teacher should have a back up plan, so that if the student's extinction burst is particularly bad, the teacher can physically remove himself/herself from the student's presence (e.g., take a break, walk away, have someone take over the classroom for a few minutes, etc.). If the behavior becomes intolerable, a precision request ("Now I need you to stop . . .") should be issued, followed by a reductive consequence if necessary.

6. The teacher should be prepared for the student to misbehave immediately after being reinforced for an appropriate behavior. This is not uncommon and is usually only temporary. It may mean that the student is seeking the teacher's negative attention, simply because it is familiar. The teacher should simply ignore the new misbehavior and try again with positive attention when it stops. This takes patience. Many Tough Kids are so used to negative attention from teachers that they prefer it to praise.

7. If differential attention with an individual student is difficult, the teacher can include another student. The teacher can ignore the Tough Kid and praise a student that is nearby (proximity praise) for appropriate behavior. When the Tough Kid behaves appropriately, then he/she can be reinforced.

Once inertia is overcome and the rock starts to roll down the hill, it picks up speed and continues to roll until it reaches the bottom. Behavioral momentum is the same. Once a series of behaviors starts to occur, they generally continue through their momentum.

Teachers can use behavioral momentum with Tough Kids, especially Tough Kids who walk into their classes with "chips on their shoulders" first thing in the morning. Behavioral momentum works by asking the Tough Kid to do two or three things the teacher knows he/she **wants to naturally** do (making a **high prob-**

ability request). The teacher should then follow this positive behavior flow with the desired low probability request. For example, a teacher can ask a Tough Kid to help pass out papers, answer a question the teacher is sure he/she knows the answer to, or help at the break. The teacher should then follow the high probability request with a lower probability behavior request, such as working on an academic assignment or cleaning his/her desk. How To Box 3-6 lists the basic steps in setting up a behavioral momentum sequence for Tough Kids.

Many Tough Kids come from difficult home environments in which they are frequently punished. Often these students have problems in the morning before they come to school. They may be punished for being slow, not being ready, or arguing with their parent(s) or siblings. In a

sense, they have a stream of punishing, low probability requests directed at them at home which has the opposite effect of positive behavioral momentum. They walk into class with a "chip on their shoulder," ready for a bad day that will only get worse. Using positive behavioral momentum first thing in the morning can help change this negative downward spiral.

It is helpful for teachers to design into their daily schedules several positive requests among the first activities of the day. Instead of reviewing the previous day's problems or having students report their progress (common practices in classrooms serving Tough Kids), several positive request activities should be substituted. For younger students, positive compliance games such as Simon Says, Seven-Up, or guessing games are good morning activities. These

How To Box 3-6

Implementing Behavioral Momentum

1. The teacher should select a series of behaviors that a student already likes to do. That is, when the teacher requests the behaviors, the student is at least 70% likely to do what the teacher requests.

2. The teacher should ask the student to do several of the **likely** behaviors before the teacher asks the student to do the behaviors he/she does not want to do (the **unlikely** behaviors). For example:

   a. "Tom, will you help me hand out the papers?";

   b. "Thanks Tom, now please help me straighten the chairs.";

   c. "Now Tom, please sit down and do your math assignment."

3. Asking two or three likely behaviors before the unlikely behavior greatly enhances the

momentum effect. However, asking even one likely behavior before the unlikely behavior can help, such as: "Tom, please help me erase the board (likely behavior). Now Tom, please write your spelling word on the board (unlikely behavior)."

4. Behavioral momentum can be engineered into the classroom schedule. Instead of starting with unlikely activities such as review of the previous day's problems, a difficult academic assignment, or calendar review, a teacher should start with likely behavior games or activities such as Simon Says, Seven-Up, team guess of a teacher's selected mystery animal, reading a high interest story, charades, etc. The teacher should then follow this activity with less likely activities (i.e., academics, problem review, etc.).

games get younger students following teachers' directions, because they are fun. For older students, listing to music, reviewing a popular magazine, or reading part of an interesting book are good morning activities. Teachers can ask questions about the music, magazine, or book as a form of positive compliance requests. These positive activities can be as short as fifteen minutes. After the positive activity, then more low probability activities such as individual seatwork or academic tasks can be assigned.

These activities can be programmed into activity schedules initially in the morning, after lunch, or after recess when compliance is frequently low and disruptive behavior is likely. The task for teachers is thinking of high probability, positive behaviors, games, and activities. To find these positive behaviors, they should watch what students naturally do, pay attention to what students frequently ask for, or simply ask students what they would like. Teachers could then incorporate these activities into their daily schedules for the whole class.

The "Sure I Will" Program

Teachers will punish a lot less if they can find an appropriate replacement behavior that interferes with the inappropriate behavior. In simpler terms, they should find a behavior they like and reward it. If the behavior interferes with arguing, noncompliance, tantrum throwing, or aggression, then these inappropriate behaviors will naturally decrease. The difficulty with noncompliance is finding an appropriate replacement behavior. The "Sure I Will" program used with precision requests allows teachers to find a replacement behavior.

If a teacher asks a student to do something, such as, "Please hand in your spelling assignment," and the student is taught to respond with the words, "Sure I Will" and begin the requested behavior, then compliance will increase. It helps

if the student is randomly rewarded for saying "Sure I Will" and the whole procedure is combined with a precision request. For example, if a precision request is made by a teacher, and the student responds with "Sure I Will" and starts the behavior before the teacher gets to "Now I **need** you to . . . ," then the teacher will receive a marked improvement in compliance (see Figure 3-7).

Saying the words, "Sure I Will" seems to help start the requested behavior and reduce arguing and noncompliance. If teachers randomly reward students for saying "Sure I Will," the improvement is even greater. For instance, with

Figure 3-7
A "Sure I Will" Request Sequence

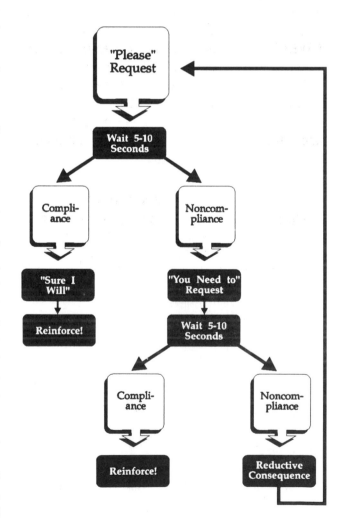

an individual student, a teacher can intermittently reward the student's saying "Sure I Will" with a social reinforcement paired with academic points or a chance to earn a small reward. Teachers should not reinforce every "Sure I Will" response, but randomly select each third or fourth response.

For whole classrooms, group contingency teams can be set up that engage in "Sure I Wills" or similar responses. A classroom can be split up into two or more teams. Each team is asked to pick a compliance phrase such as, "Sure I Will," "Okey Dokey," "Glad You Asked," "Sure Any Time," "No Problem," etc. The teams are listed on the blackboard and checks are put by each team's name for their individual compliance responses (see Figure 3-8). It is important for the teacher to begin the "Sure I Will" program by giving checks to teams and praising liberally when the students respond with "Sure I Will" or their other assigned compliance responses. When the program really starts to take hold (i.e., in two or three days), then the teacher should increase the criteria and give checks only for genuine responses or exceptional performance. It is important, at that point, to randomly reward only the most genuine "Sure I Will"-type responses.

The teams' checks can be exchanged for a chance at a Mystery Motivator or some other privilege. For example, the teacher can write down a secret number. At the end of each day the number can be read to the class, and if a team's number of checks on the blackboard is the same or greater than the secret number, then the team receives the Mystery Motivator. Again, once the program takes hold, then the secret number can be read every two or three days instead of every day. This helps improve student performance over the long term.

The "Sure I Will" program can also be combined with a response cost procedure to make it even more effective. For example, one check by a team's name on the blackboard can be erased if a student from that team misbehaves. For instance, if a student goes to time out, a check can be erased. Or, if a student does not respond to a precision request after the **need** statement, then a check can be erased. It is important that the response cost option be used only rarely. The "Sure I Will" program should primarily be a positive program, not a program that threatens or frequently punishes students. If checks are often erased for the behavior of a particular student, the teacher should determine that the student can actually perform the behavior or determine that the potency of the reward is adequate.

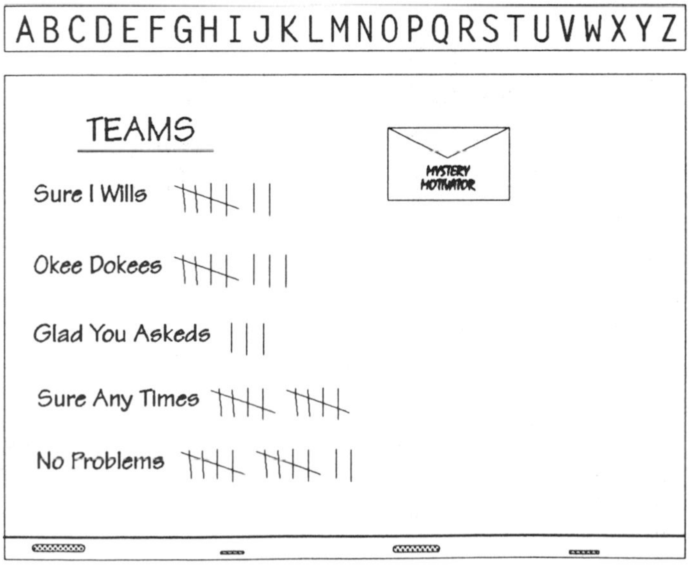

One word of caution when using the "Sure I Will" program. Preliminary research has found the program to be exceptionally efficient at improving compliance (Martin-LeMaster, 1990). The problem is that repeated "Sure I Wills" can become tiring and repetitive. One teacher complained that high rate, repeated "Sure I Wills" are tedious. No one has complained about the compliance

Figure 3-8
Blackboard Example of "Sure I Will" Program Teams

rates, just the high rates and repetition of the same compliance response. To solve this problem, a teacher should require students (or teams) to vary their compliance responses. Once they master one compliance response, students should choose another (see examples above), and then another. When they are proficient with them all, then they can give the teacher a different one each time they respond. This varied approach makes the response seem far more natural.

How To Box 3-7 summarizes the steps in implementing the "Sure I Will" program.

The Compliance Matrix

Some activities are naturally rewarding: One likes the process of participating in the activity almost as much as one likes the reward or outcome. Bingo is such an activity. It is a popular game, widely used by social organizations and churches, and it is a naturally rewarding activity in itself. The Compliance Matrix is a variation of Bingo that can be used to dramatically improve classroom compliance (Jesse, 1990). The word matrix (a square composed of several equal sized cells) sounds more scientific than Bingo (a popular game in which players use matrix cards to win prizes).

The Compliance Matrix requires the following materials: a series of matrices with numbered cells (see Figure 3-9) drawn on an erasable whiteboard, numbered objects (e.g., White, round cardboard key tags, available from office supply stores, work great. Other options are small pink erasers, poker chips, or checkers numbered with permanent marker, or even slips of paper.) that equal the number of cells in the matrix currently used, and an opaque container to hold the numbered objects. When a student follows a command, he/she is allowed to draw one of the numbered objects from the container. The student is not allowed to peek and select a numbered object, but must randomly draw one.

The number which is drawn is marked (with a water-based marker) on his/her matrix board, and when any row, column, or any diagonal is completed, the student earns a reinforcer (e.g., Mystery Motivator, Spinner, etc.).

To use the Compliance Matrix practically in a classroom, several modifications or suggestions can make the procedure more effective. First, it is easier to use the matrix with a group contingency. Have one large Compliance Matrix at the front of the classroom that can be used to reinforce the whole class (also, it helps to hang a Mystery Motivator next to the matrix to build up expectation). For example, when the criteria is met, the whole class receives the reward at the next free time break or recess. However, if students complain about the reward or ask for something else, they lose the reward altogether.

Second, several teams can be used with the matrix and a group contingency. Each team can be assigned a color (e.g., Red Team, Blue Team, Green Team, etc.), and the team's color can be marked in the matrix cell of the drawn number whenever a student of that team complies to the teacher's requests. Several teams can occupy the same cell if they randomly draw that cell's number (e.g., red, blue, and green X's could all be written in cell number five). The advantage of this approach is that teams compete to be compliant and follow the classroom rules. In addition, all the teams can win. If, at any time, a team member tries to sabotage the rest of the team's effort, that student should be made a team by himself/herself.

Third, it helps to combine the Compliance Matrix with precision requests. For example, a student (or team member) can draw a number only if he/she responds when the teacher first issues the "Please" request. If the student waits until the teacher reaches the "I need you to . . . " statement, he/she is not allowed to draw a number from the container. Combining precision requests with the Compliance Matrix enhances both programs.

How To Box 3-7

Implementing the "Sure I Will" Program

The "Sure I Will" program is based on the idea that if a student verbally responds to a teacher's request with "Sure I Will," then he/she is less likely to be noncompliant. In a sense, the "Sure I Will" response interferes with noncompliance.

1. The "Sure I Will" program is used with precision requests. The student must respond to a teacher's "Please" request with "Sure I Will" and start the behavior before the teacher issues the second request with the word **need** ("Now I need you to . . . "). If the student waits, he/she is not rewarded.

2. The student's "Sure I Will" response should always be socially rewarded by the teacher.

3. The student may also be rewarded randomly with a tangible reward such as academic points or a small toy.

4. The "Sure I Will" program can best be used with teams and a group contingency by following these steps:

    a. Each classroom team has a special response (e.g., "Sure I Will", "Okey Dokey", "Glad You Asked," "Sure Any Time," "No Problem," etc.).

    b. The teacher selects a secret number each day that is unknown to the students (i.e., One day it might be 20, then 15, then 19.) and writes it down on a piece of paper.

    c. The team's names are posted on the blackboard.

    d. The teacher makes a chalk mark by each team's name when a team member responds with his/her team's preselected verbal response and begins the behavior. For example, "Jeffery, please sit down in your seat."; "Sure I will, Mrs. Johnson," and he sits down.

    e. When the program first starts, the teacher should be liberal in recording marks for teams. However, after several days the teacher should only accept genuine efforts or sincere responses.

    f. At the end of each day, the teacher announces the secret number. If the number of a team's marks is the same or bigger than the secret number, the team gets to participate in the class reward (e.g., Mystery Motivator or Grab-Bag).

    g. If a team's number of marks is less than the secret number, they continue to do what is normally scheduled at that time of the day.

Figure 3-9
Examples of Compliance Matrices

A.

1	2	3
4	5	6
7	8	9

B.

1	2	3	4
5	6	7	8
9	10	11	12
13	14	15	16

C.

1	2	3	4	5
6	7	8	9	10
11	12	13	14	15
16	17	18	19	20
21	22	23	24	25

can also use the program to shape on-task behavior (i.e., let a student draw a number when he/she is really concentrating) or to catch a student being particularly good and following the classroom rules.

The Compliance Matrix program can be gradually thinned by using bigger and bigger matrices. Start with the simple three by three matrix (see Figure 3-9, Panel A). When the students are stable and doing well move to the four by four matrix (see Figure 3-9, Panel B), and finally to the five by five matrix (see Figure 3-9, Panel C).

Another method of thinning the compliance Matrix program is to use duplicate numbered items in the container. If a student draws a numbered item that has already been drawn, then the item is returned to the container and the student is praised for doing a good job.

An unmarked "wild card" item may be placed in the container to add interest to the technique. If this wild card item is drawn, the student is entitled to select any number in the matrix to be marked. A different wild card item may also be added to the container which, if drawn, will permit all teams that have earned at least one mark on the matrix and have not lost any marks for misbehavior to earn the designated reward at the next break.

It also helps to improve the Compliance Matrix program if teachers learn to use the Compliance Matrix to shape behavior. If the teacher allows students to draw numbers each time they comply to a request, the matrix will fill up too fast. At first, the teacher can be liberal in allowing them to draw numbers. However, over time the program should be thinned and only one response in every four or five should be rewarded. At this point, the teacher should inform the students that they can draw a number from the container only when the teacher believes they have done a particularly good job. The teacher

The Compliance Matrix program can also be used in combination with a response cost procedure. This is particularly effective when the program is used with the group contingency option explained above. For example, if a student defies a teacher's request, then an X can be erased from the team's matrix. Similarly, if a student goes to time out, blatantly breaks a classroom rule, or defies the teacher an X can be erased. The response cost option with the Compliance Matrix should be used sparingly.

How To Box 3-8 summarizes the steps in implementing the Compliance Matrix program.

How To Box 3-8

Implementing the Compliance Matrix Program

The Compliance Matrix is really a game patterned after Bingo that can be used in a classroom to improve student compliance to teacher requests.

1. The basic materials needed to implement the procedure are:

    a.   a set of matrices (see Figure 3-9), drawn on an erasable whiteboard;

    b.   small items that can be numbered;

    c.   an opaque container to hold the items;

    d.   water-based color markers; and

    e.   a reward system such as a Mystery Motivator, Spinner, or reinforcer menu.

2. The matrix is posted at the front of the classroom. It helps if the matrix is large (3 ft X 3 ft is desirable). The water-based pen(s) should be kept near the matrix for easy use.

3. The reward system is posted next to the matrix (e.g., the Mystery Motivator envelope or the Spinner).

4. The small items are marked with the numbers corresponding to the cells in the matrix. A matrix with nine numbered cells would at least have nine items marked with the numbers one to nine.

5. The items are placed in the container and the teacher keeps them handy.

6. When a student complies to the teacher's requests, is following the classroom rules, or is on-task studying, the teacher asks the student to look away and draw an item at random from the container.

7. The number on the drawn item is marked on the matrix with the water-based pen.

8. When any row, column, or diagonal is complete, the class receives the reward at the next free time break or recess (the Mystery Motivator or the right to spin the reinforcement Spinner). If students complain about the reward or want something else, they lose the reward.

9. The matrix board is then erased and the game is started over.

10. When students are responding to teacher commands at high rates, the next matrix is introduced (the four by four, and finally the five by five). The larger matrices thin the reward schedule for the teacher.

11. It helps not to allow the students to draw items each time they comply or are working well. Instead, the teacher should randomly allow students to draw. When the procedure is first started, the teacher can be liberal in allowing them to draw numbers. Over time, only about one in four or five good student responses should earn a draw.

12. Teachers can use duplicate items in the container to help thin out the reward schedule even more. For example, if a student draws a numbered item that has already been drawn and marked on the matrix, then the item is simply replaced in the container and the student is congratulated for doing a good job.

13. It helps to have an unmarked wild card item, that if drawn, entitles the student to pick any number in the matrix that he/she wants marked.

14. Another type of wild card item may also be included. If this item is drawn, all teams that have at least one mark on the matrix and have not had a number erased for misbehavior will win at the next break.

15. The compliance matrix works exceptionally well as a group contingency. Teams can be assigned colors (Red Team, Blue Team, Green Team, etc.) and each team assigned a water-based colored pen. When a team member draws a number, the number's corresponding matrix cell is marked with the color of the student's team. Several colors can be marked in the same cell. Individual teams compete to win. Teams with a row, column, or diagonal completed receive the reward at the next break. Teams that do not win do not receive the reward at the next break.

16. If a team member tries to sabotage his/her team's genuine effort, that student can be made a team by himself/herself.

17. A response cost procedure can be used with the Compliance Matrix. If students misbehave, are off-task, or break a class rule, then a marked number on the matrix can be erased. This works well with teams, particularly if a team has already won and know they will receive the reward at the next break. If a team member misbehaves, then the team win can be lost because a number is erased.

Summary

A reductive technique is any research-valid procedure that temporarily stops or suppresses a behavior. The emphasis in this chapter has been on research-valid techniques. If there is no research evidence to support the use and effectiveness of a reductive technique, then teachers are at risk professionally and ethically when using them.

Another emphasis in this chapter is that reductive techniques only temporarily suppress a misbehavior. They can give a teacher a "window of opportunity" to build in more functional social, academic, and self-management behaviors to replace the maladaptive behavior. If behaviors are merely suppressed with a reductive technique, and students are not taught appropriate behaviors to replace them, then the misbehavior will reappear.

Reductive techniques generally produce a rapid temporary behavior change that rewards their implementers and often results in their overuse. These procedures should be used sparingly with Tough Kids who make teaching difficult and disrupt the class. It is very easy to overuse punishment, which results in students disliking teachers and the educational setting in general. This chapter has presented several alternative positive programs that can be used to improve classroom compliance. Techniques such as the "Sure I Will" program, the Compliance Matrix, and maximizing antecedents through precision request are all positive procedures that can used by teachers to improve compliance. If possible, these approaches should be used first and a major emphasis should be placed on positive replacement techniques.

If reductive techniques are required, teachers should be familiar with variables that allow them to use the procedures precisely and for the shortest possible period of time. Effectiveness variables reviewed in this chapter include establishing the teacher as likeable and highly rewarding. Reductive techniques applied by someone students like is far more effective than from someone they dislike. It is also important for teachers to reward appropriate behaviors that actually interfere with misbehaviors. For example, the "Sure I Will" program presented in this chapter actively interferes with noncompliance and is a highly valued behavior in and of itself. Using reductive techniques early on in an aversive behavior chain also makes them far more effective. If the teacher waits until the student is out of control and at the peak of a misbehavior, then intervening becomes far less effective. Similarly, optimizing the antecedent variables of request making (i.e., no questions, the distance factor, eye contact, requesting only twice, remaining nonemotional, and making more start than stop requests) maximizes the use of several reductive procedures.

Preplanning, consistency, and unique applications are the keys to using reductive procedures sparingly but effectively. Preplanning with a hierarchy of reductive consequences helps to avoid selecting a consequence in the heat of a coercive interaction with a student. When teachers select a consequence during one of these coercive interactions, they tend to use overly harsh or unrealistic reductive consequences. A publicly posted **What If? Chart** that lists a hierarchy of reductive consequences for increasingly difficult misbehaviors is a good approach. The chart should also contain a serious behavior clause (i.e., procedures to temporarily remove a student from the classroom) for crisis or out-of-control behavior episodes. The **What If? Chart** should also contain a list of rewards for appropriate behaviors (i.e., no rule infractions for the day, everyone handing in their homework, perfect recess behavior, etc.).

Unique procedures reduce the need to use reductive techniques with Tough Kids. Simple but creative procedures such as differential attention, behavioral momentum, the Compliance Matrix, or Bumpy Bunny Time Out are procedures that students appear to enjoy. Enjoyment of the educational process is what is lacking in most Tough Kid's lives. These students have long histories of academic failure, have been overly punished for their misbehaviors, and have experienced rejection from peers. To help motivate them to come to school, behave appropriately, learn new social skills, and achieve academically is the essence of the goals of a good classroom. Reductive procedures may be necessary, but they should be used sparingly and as an adjunct to a behavior-building, positive core program.

References

Forehand, R. (1977). Child noncompliance to parental requests: Behavior analysis and treatment. In M. Hersen, R.M. Eisler, & P.M. Miller (Eds.), *Progress in behavior modification* (Vol. 5) (pp. 111-148). New York: Academic Press.

Hamlet, C.C., Axelrod, S., & Kuerschner, S. (1984). Eye contact as an antecedent to compliant behavior. *Journal of Applied Behavior Analysis, 17,* 553-557.

Jesse, V.C. (1990). *Compliance training and generalization effects using a compliance matrix and spinner system.* Unpublished dissertation, University of Utah, Salt Lake City, UT.

Martin-LeMaster, J. (1990). *Increasing classroom compliance of noncompliant elementary age students.* Unpublished dissertation, University of Utah, Salt Lake City, UT.

Patterson, G.R. (1976). The aggressive child: Victim and architect of a coercive system. In E.J. Mash, L.A. Hamerlynck, & L.C. Handy (Eds.), *Behavior modification and families* (pp. 267-316). New York: Brunner Mazel.

Proctor, M.A. & Morgan, D. (1991). Effectiveness of a response cost raffle procedure on the disruptive classroom behavior of adolescents with behavior problems. *School Psychology Review, 20,* 97-109.

Van Houten, R. & Doleys, D. (1983). Are social reprimands effective? In S. Axelrod and J. Apsche (Eds.), *The effects of punishment on human behavior* (pp. 45-70). New York: Academic Press.

White, M.A. (1975). Natural rates of teacher approval and disapproval in the classroom. *Journal of Applied Behavior Analysis, 8,* 111-120.

Witt, J.C. & Elliot, S.N. (1982). The response cost lottery: A time efficient and effective classroom intervention. *Journal of School Psychology, 20,* 155-161.

Chapter 4

Advanced Systems for Tough Kids

Advanced systems are designed for use with the most difficult students teachers will have in their classrooms. It is estimated that one to two percent of the school population will require the use of advanced systems. These procedures are extremely powerful in changing the behavior of students with severe behavior problems.

A basic assumption in using any advanced system is that those students for which it is being considered are in a classroom setting with a correctly implemented basic management system in place. It is assumed that the teacher has already adjusted the basic classroom management system and found it to be ineffective in meeting the needs of these students. This is important for two reasons. First, many students exhibit severe behavior problems as a result of ineffective, dysfunctional classroom management. These are students whose behavior could be managed with a consistent, basic management approach. When this is absent, the inappropriate behaviors of these students escalate. In this case, the real problem is a teacher problem rather than a student problem. Second, the goal for all Tough Kids is to sufficiently change their behavior so that ultimately they can be effectively taught using the basic classroom management plan. Ideally, teachers will not want to use the more intrusive advanced systems indefinitely if students can be taught to work within the basic

classroom management system. If this system is not in place, obviously there is nothing to maintain the positive behavior changes once advanced systems are faded from use. Various advanced systems will be described in detail in this chapter.

"Drastic Measures"

In addition to classroom management issues, Tough Kids often experience difficulty in the area of academic instruction. Sometimes so much effort and energy are devoted to managing their behavior that their academic instruction is not given careful consideration. In designing effective, advanced systems for Tough Kids, their academic instruction must also be taken into account.

Academic Instruction

An appropriate approach to teaching Tough Kids is one in which the behavior management they require is planned and implemented within the context of teaching them the academic skills they need. Without improvement of academic skills, even the most "advanced" behavior management system will not decrease behavior problems over the long term.

It is a fact that many Tough Kids are significantly behind their peers when it comes to academic performance, particularly in the area of reading. Since reading is so critical to a great deal of learning, reading programs should be assessed very carefully for Tough Kids who have a history of learning difficulties. Guidelines for providing reading instruction for these students are provided in How To Box 4-1.

Academic Learning Time

The effective schools literature tells educators to minimize the amount of class time spent on "housekeeping" tasks. The majority should be spent on academic instruction. Assuming that the Tough Kid is skill deficient, the amount of academic learning time in his/her program is absolutely critical, since rapid progress is essential to improvement.

Academic learning time refers to the amount of time students are actually engaged in, and experiencing success in, learning. The time must be spent on learning essential skills the Tough Kid needs to acquire. Obviously, if academic learning time is spent on meaningless tasks, it will not be highly related to learning. Increased achievement will occur only if time is spent on appropriate instruction. To achieve a level of academic learning time of no less than 70%, teachers must address several variables, detailed in How To Box 4-2.

How To Box 4-1

Reading Program Guidelines for Tough Kids

Extra Instruction

- The more deficient the student is, the more extra instruction he/she should be receiving.

Early Remediation

- Help should be made available as early as possible to be effective.

Careful Instruction

- Instruction must be more exacting in relation to the severity of the reading deficits.

Well-Designed Program

- A program which focuses on essential skills is crucial.

Rapid Progression

- The greater the student's deficits, the more rapid his/her progress must be.

Motivation

- Progress and success are in direct proportion to the student's motivation.

Source: Carnine & Silbert (1979).

Increasing Academic Learning Time

To increase academic learning time, several variables must be addressed by the teacher.

Begin on Time

- While a simple concept, many teachers lose valuable instructional time by beginning class (or tasks) late. It is important for the teacher to reinforce the expectation of beginning on time and recognize and reward those students who meet that expectation.

Minimize "Housekeeping" Tasks

- The teacher must be ever alert for ways to streamline the everyday "housekeeping" tasks which take away from instructional time. Simplifying tasks and having students assist with those which are necessary are helpful.

Minimize Transition Time

- A great deal of time can be wasted if the transition between different academic learning activities is not managed efficiently and smoothly. Transition time can be minimized by:
  - having materials organized and ready;
  - confidently closing one activity and initiating the next;
  - increasing monitoring of students during transition times (praising and recognizing those who transition quickly); and
  - planning activities at which students **can** succeed, so that they will be enthusiastic about beginning the next activity.

Direct Instruction

Research indicates overwhelming support for the use of direct instruction (DI) to teach basic skills to hard to teach students. While Tough Kids are not specifically included in direct instruction research, the methods incorporated in direct instruction are well-suited for use with them. Not only are the teaching strategies themselves applicable for Tough Kids, but direct instruction maximizes academic learning time and provides a very structured learning environment where Tough Kids simply do not have the opportunity to disrupt and engage in misbehavior.

It is important for teachers to know that there is no single type of direct instruction; in fact, some are considerably more "direct" than others. What is indicated, however, is that the more direct the instruction, the more effective it is and that more direct instructional time is associated with greater achievement.

Direct instruction is an instructional approach that emphasizes the use of group instruction and face-to-face instruction by teachers or aides us-

ing carefully sequenced lessons. Many direct instruction programs have the following characteristics:

- Teacher presentations are scripted and preplanned.
- Presentations are fast paced.
- Small groups are utilized to maximize student response opportunities and teacher monitoring.
- Oral group responding is incorporated to monitor the ongoing learning of all students.
- Skills are taught to mastery.
- Individual mastery tests are administered to confirm mastery.
- Student motivation is maintained by teacher praise and encouragement and other reinforcement.
- When students make errors, correction is immediate, using specific correction procedures.

Pointer Box 4-1 lists available commercial instructional materials recommended for a direct instruction approach to academic instruction.

Recommended Direct Instruction Programs*

MATH

Connecting Math Concepts, Levels A-D (grades 1-4)

- Program designed to ensure that all students will learn higher order thinking and mathematics; establishes relationships among concepts and their application, introduces concepts at a reasonable rate and provides systematic, continuous review so that students learn, remember, and integrate the concepts they are taught. Components include a teacher's guide and presentation books, separate answer key, student workbooks, and student textbooks at Levels C and D.

Corrective Mathematics (grades 3-12)

- Designed for students who have not mastered basic arithmetic skills. The four modules—Addition, Subtraction, Multiplication, and Division—may be used separately or in combination. Each is designed to teach effective strategies for learning and retaining facts, solving computational problems, and translating story problems into numerical statements. Preskill and placement tests in each module place students into the program and direct students only to lessons they need. Mastery tests are also built into the program. Components for each module include a teacher presentation book, a separate answer key, and a student book.

Distar Arithmetic I and *II* (preschool through grade 2)

- Effectively teaches strategies for learning and retaining facts, solving computational problems, and working story problems. The program breaks complex tasks into component skills, teaching preskills, and demonstrating how the components are combined. Components at each level include a classroom lab with teacher's guide, student workbooks, behavioral objectives, skills profile folders, and mastery tests.

Mathematics Modules (grades 4-adult)

- Modules on basic fractions, fractions, decimals, percentages, ratios, and equations can be used with individuals or an entire class. Pretests provide for accurate placement, and a lesson-skipping schedule keeps students moving at their own pace. Components in each module include a teacher presentation book with separate answer key and student workbooks.

READING

Corrective Reading (grades 3-12)

- Program designed for students who haven't learned in other programs and don't learn on their own. It includes core programs for decoding and comprehension. Components include teacher presentation books, student books for decoding and comprehension, workbooks, mastery tests, and a series guide.

Distar Language I-III (preschool through grade 3)

- Teaches foundation skills for reading comprehension, and focuses on expressive and receptive language and cognitive development. Is useful in classes where English is not students' primary language. Components vary depending upon program level.

Pointer Box 4-1 cont'd

Reading Mastery I-VI (grades 1-6)

- Comprehensive program systematically teaches phonics, critical thinking, and comprehension strategies. Components include teacher guides, presentation books, storybooks and textbooks, workbooks and skillbooks, testing and management systems, behavioral objectives and skills profile charts, and a series guide.

Reading Mastery: Fast Cycle (for faster learners in grades K-1 or "catch-up" in grades 2-3)

- Program covers all the basic word-attack and comprehension skills of *Reading Mastery I* and *II* at a faster pace with less repetition and drill. Program components include a teacher's guide, four presentation books, spelling book, storybooks, workbooks, group progress indicators, behavioral objectives, and a skills profile folder.

SPELLING

Corrective Spelling Through Morphographs (grades 4-adult)

- Program is designed for students who have failed to learn through other spelling approaches. This intensive one-year program leads to spelling of over 12,000 words, including most problem words. It teaches basic units of meaning in written language that are always spelled according to specific rules. Components include a teacher's book, student book with exercise sheets, progress charts, and student-teacher contract. Blackline master exercises are also available.

Spelling Mastery (grades 1-6)

- Program emphasizes learning to spell by generalization rather than by weekly memorization of word lists. Teaches students to apply phonemic, morphemic, and whole word strategies to what they write. Program components at each level include a teacher's book (with placement test), student workbook, and series guide.

WRITING

Basic Writing Skills (grades 4-8)

- Teaches students who are deficient in primary writing skills to compose coherent, understandable, and correctly written sentences. Students learn rules of capitalization and punctuation as well as how to recognize and write a complete sentence.

Cursive Writing Program (grades 3-4)

- Program offers a structured approach for students who have already mastered manuscript writing. Students learn to form letters, create words, write sentences, and improve their speed and accuracy.

Expressive Writing I and II (grades 4-6)

- Program for students who read at least at third grade level and read and write cursive. Students learn to develop sentence and paragraph skills, editing, and component skills. Program components include a teacher presentation book with goals and objectives, pretest, lesson presentation instructions, and student workbooks.

*These products are all available from:
Science Research Associates (SRA) • School Group • 155 North Wacker Drive • Chicago, IL 60606

Monitoring and Evaluation of Academic Progress

Because most Tough Kids have no time to lose in making academic progress, it is essential that regular monitoring and evaluation take place. It is insufficient for teachers to record unsatisfactory scores and grades week after week and then to conclude at the end of the year that the students were unsuccessful.

Achievement tests can provide feedback to teachers once or twice a year but are insufficient for ongoing monitoring and evaluation. At least weekly or biweekly mini tests or mastery tests which are keyed to the instructional programs in use are essential. Thus, if a student hasn't mastered the skill(s) just taught, the teacher knows right away that additional instruction must be provided. If the Tough Kid is not sufficiently motivated to do his/her best in learning new skills, the teacher will also need to provide effective positive reinforcement for learning them.

Cooperative Learning Strategies

Cooperative learning strategies are appealing for use with Tough Kids for a number of reasons: (1) they have been shown to increase achievement, especially in low-achieving students; (2) they have been shown to be helpful in successfully mainstreaming Tough Kids; (3) they promote positive social relations and development; and (4) they have been shown to increase students' affection for themselves, each other, class, school, and learning.

Cooperative learning consists of dividing the class into small teams of students who are made interdependent upon each other, in a positive way, by the use of a reward and/or task structure. Procedures for using cooperative learning are described in How To Box 4-3.

With cooperative learning, students are most often evaluated with individual quizzes so that the teacher can continue to monitor individual progress. Students generally earn points for their teams based on improvement over past performance.

The teacher then uses newsletters, bulletin boards, and other social rewards and forms of recognition for teams' performance. Recognition of individuals who have performed extremely well or who have made sufficient improvement is also important.

"An Uncooperative Learner"

How To Box 4-3

Cooperative Learning Procedures

1. Identify the academic objectives and cooperative learning objectives (e.g., social/cooperative skills) to be taught and recognized.

2. Decide on the size of the groups, composition of groups, how long the groups will function (a week, month, etc.), and the physical arrangement of the classroom.

3. Assign roles to group members (e.g., checker, accuracy coach, team manager, cheerleader); emphasize to group members that their team is collaborative and that they are reliant upon one another for success or failure.

4. Explain the learning task and cooperative goal structure to the students. The cooperative goal structure usually includes a group goal, criteria for success, an understanding that all group members receive the same grade, an awareness of the cooperative learning skills required for the task, and a reminder that it is desirable to assist other groups in the classroom.

5. Monitor and intervene as needed as students work collaboratively. Provide assistance when called for.

6. Evaluate individual student learning, group products, and individual and group cooperative learning/collaboration skills.

Sources: Johnson D.W. & Johnson, R.T. (1980); Johnson, D.W. & Johnson, R.T. (1986).

Social Skills Training

By definition, Tough Kids exhibit significant social skills deficiencies when they are compared with their successful peers. There are those who propose that students with severe behavior problems need only spend time with their normal peers to learn the desired skills. However, Tough Kids are poorly accepted by their "normal" peers, resulting in minimal interaction between them even when they do spend time together. When interaction does occur, it is often negative. It becomes clear that if all that was needed was to expose Tough Kids to their normal peers in order for them to acquire appropriate social skills, they would have acquired acceptable social skills already.

Lack of appropriate social skills not only affects Tough Kids while they are in school, but extends into their adult lives as well. Students who are noncompliant, disruptive, and act out during their school years grow up to be noncompliant adults with similar problems. As a group, they have multiple marriages, difficulty holding jobs, and break society's laws. It is clear that if these problems are not addressed during their school years, the students and society as a whole will suffer their effects indefinitely.

Many Tough Kids also lack the minimal behavior skills necessary to promote their academic learning. Research indicates that most teachers have fairly rigid standards of behavior to which students are expected to conform. When students fail to do this, the whole learning process is disrupted, and their classroom success is impeded. Thus, it is essential that Tough Kids receive specific social skills training in their

school programs to break this cycle of failure. When Tough Kids have not acquired necessary social skills vicariously, they must be taught them directly, with a focus on specific problem areas.

The most effective social skills training programs for Tough Kids use a direct instruction approach, incorporating many of the same components used with academic programs. These components are described in Box 4-1.

Box 4-1

Components of Effective Social Skills Programs

Instructions and Rationales

- Students are informed about the specific skills they will be taught and how the skills will help them be more successful in daily interactions. A definition of the skills and examples of them are provided.

Modeling

- Modeling can be incorporated by using films or videotapes, audio cassette tapes, live demonstrations, puppets, books, or mental imagery.

Concept Teaching

- Concept teaching involves presenting the critical and irrelevant attributes of a social skill concept and determining whether the student can distinguish between **examples** and **nonexamples** of the concept. Examples of a skill might include a videotape depicting several scenes of the skill "doing what the teacher asks promptly." Nonexamples might include videotape depictions of students **not** "doing what the teacher asks promptly."

Role Playing/Behavior Rehearsal and Practice

- The student rehearses how to behave in situations that have caused difficulty in the past or may cause difficulty in the future. The teacher may first model the appropriate behavior and then provide prompts, coaching, and feedback to the student during the rehearsal. As is the case with any skill, the amount and quality of practice time is a critical variable in acquiring it.

Coaching

- Coaching involves verbally instructing students by focusing on relevant cues, concepts, and rules.

Contingent Reinforcement

- Teachers must know how and when to praise, ignore, and give students corrective feedback to effectively teach social skills. A positive reinforcement system will probably be required to help Tough Kids acquire and maintain the social skills they need to learn.

There are a number of very effective social skills programs on the market which can be incorporated into the Tough Kid's school program to directly teach needed social skills. Pointer Box 4-2 provides information regarding recommended social skills programs. All those listed have been well researched and their effectiveness documented when used as directed by the publisher.

There is no doubt that even Tough Kids can be taught social skills within the confines of four classroom walls. The real trick is to get them to use the social skills that they are taught in the classroom **in other settings**. It is a big mistake for teachers to assume that Tough Kids will exhibit social skills in other settings once they have been taught to use them in the classroom. There are a number of procedures that teachers must incorporate in order to encourage the generalized use of social skills by Tough Kids to other settings where they are needed and desired. How To Box 4-4 outlines these procedures.

How To Box 4-4

Procedures to Enhance Social Skills Generalization

- Teach behaviors that will maximize success and minimize failure. (Teach behaviors that are needed and will be used in other settings.)
- Make the classroom training realistic by using relevant examples and nonexamples. Role play and rehearsal activities should reflect what actually happens in students' lives.
- Make sure students learn the skills in the classroom training part of the program. The teacher must provide lots of supervised practice opportunities.
- Provide social skills "homework" assignments. This will allow the students opportunities to practice outside the classroom setting.
- Require a self-report following a homework assignment. Provide positive reinforcement for accuracy of the self-report and the actual achievement of the homework assignment. If a student has failed at either of these, the teacher should utilize problem-solving strategies to resolve them before the next training session.

- Program the other settings to support the new skills, whenever possible. Other school staff, peers, and parents must help reinforce and prompt newly learned social skills.
- Gradually fade special positive reinforcement programs to eventually approximate the actual reinforcement available in real life.
- Teach self-management skills to help the student maintain improved social skills (See the Self-Management section of this chapter.)
- For more difficult cases, the teacher may need to go the extra mile and actually follow the students into other settings to prompt, coach, correct, and reinforce new skills. The teacher then fades out of the outside settings.
- Use periodic "booster sessions" if the students' behavior deteriorates or as a preventive measure. Reteach or review appropriate lessons.

Source: Morgan & Jenson (1988).

Recommended Social Skills Programs

Elementary Populations

Getting Along With Others: Teaching Social Effectiveness to Children. Jackson, N.F., Jackson, D.A., & Monroe, C. (1983). Champaign, IL: Research Press.
  • Program guide (126 pages), $12.95; skill lessons and activities, $21.95; complete set, $29.95. Program lists 17 skills and the steps needed to teach them. Each lesson includes role plays, relaxation training, activities, and homework assignments.

Skillstreaming the Elementary School Child. McGinnis, E. & Goldstein, A.P. (1984). Champaign, IL: Research Press.
  • Program guide (254 pages), $13.95. Program covers 60 specific prosocial skills such as saying thank you, asking for help, apologizing, dealing with anger, responding to teasing, and handling group pressure. Addresses the needs of students who display aggression, immaturity, withdrawal, and other problem behaviors.

The Walker Social Skills Curriculum: The ACCEPTS Program. Walker, H.M., McConnell, S., Holmes, D., Todis, B., Walker, J., & Golden, N. (1983). Austin, TX: Pro-Ed Publishing Co.
  • Curriculum guide (160 pages), $22.00. Includes nine step instructional procedure based on principals of direct instruction, scripts for teaching, and placement test.

Secondary Populations

Adolescent Coping Curriculum for Effective Social Skills (ACCESS). Walker, H.M., Todis, J., Holmes, D., & Horton, D. (1988). Austin, TX: Pro-Ed Publishing Co.
  • Program includes a teacher's guide (137 pages), student guide, and role playing cards, $34.00. Twenty-eight lessons cover 15 social skills. Contracting and self-reporting are utilized to transfer newly learned skills to other school settings.

Aggression Replacement Training. Goldstein, A.P. & Glick, B. (1987). Champaign, IL: Research Press.
  • Program guide (376 pages), $17.95. Group program designed to teach adolescents to understand and replace aggression with positive alternatives.

The Prepare Curriculum. Goldstein, A.P. (1988). Champaign, IL: Research Press.
  • Program guide (700 pages), $27.95. Designed for use with students who are chronically aggressive, withdrawn or otherwise weak in prosocial competencies. The curriculum includes ten course-length interventions: Problem Solving, Interpersonal Skills, Situational Perception, Anger Control, Moral Reasoning, Stress Management, Empathy, Recruit Supportive Models, Cooperation, and Understanding and Using Groups.

Skillstreaming the Adolescent. Goldstein, A.P., Sprafkin, R.P., Gershaw, N.J., & Klein, P. (1980). Champaign, IL: Research Press.
  • Program guide (232 pages), $13.95. Program provides training in 50 prosocial skills such as expressing feelings, maintaining a conversation, setting a goal, apologizing, responding to teasing, and standing up for oneself or a friend. Appropriate for students who display aggression, immaturity, or withdrawal.

Public Posting

Public Posting is a strategy which may be effectively used with Tough Kids to decrease disruptive behaviors and improve academic motivation. It consists of posting measures of behavior or academic progress scores on a conspicuous bulletin board or blackboard in the classroom. Postings for behavior may include being on time to class, being prepared to work, appropriate transitions from class to class, improved citizenship scores, number of points earned for appropriate behavior, and so on. Academic postings may include scores on assignments and tests, number of assignments completed on time, handwriting samples, story writing, and contributions made in class.

In order for Public Posting to be effective, several components are essential:

- Some type of visual feedback system must be present and must be visible from students' desks. A conspicuous bulletin board, blackboard, poster, or display case are all appropriate for public posting.

- Accurate and meaningful information must be publicly posted. The more recent the information and the more immediately it is posted, the more effective the public posting will be.

- An engineered reaction to the posting is very important. This refers to the responses of other school personnel, peers, the principal, and parents to the public posting system. Since public posting usually has no other reward associated with it other than the fact that it is prominently displayed, the positively reinforcing reaction of others is critical. If this is not likely to happen naturally, the teacher will need to do everything possible to structure it.

In order to effectively implement a public posting system, the steps listed below are recommended:

Step 1: Select a **visual feedback system** to be prominently displayed in the classroom so that students can see it from their desks. Lettering should be large and bold. It is suggested that charts be erasable (e.g., laminated poster board), and contain a week's worth of data (Monday through Friday). Keep the system simple!

Step 2: Decide on a **positive improvement** to post. Students should be compared against their own performance, rather than against each other. Thus, improvement is emphasized.

Step 3: Decide on a **specific, meaningful daily measure**, such as daily points earned for appropriate behavior.

Step 4: Give feedback **immediately**. The more immediately the feedback is given, the more effective the posting system will be.

Step 5: Develop a system to score or evaluate the students' work or behavior so that it can be posted immediately. Self or peer grading/rating can be used rather than waiting for the teacher to do the grading.

Method 1: Give students special colored pencils or pens for grading to prevent cheating. The teacher may randomly grade papers for accuracy after students have graded them.

Method 2: Set up grading stations with answer sheets and special colored pencils or pens for grading. Students are allowed to bring only their answer sheets to the grading station. No other pencils or papers are allowed.

Method 3: Have students exchange papers and put their initials at the bottom as the grader. It may help to have students rotate papers two or three times so that students are not next to their graders. Again, the teacher can randomly grade a few papers after students have graded them to check for accuracy.

Step 6: Give positive feedback for student improvements against their own best scores, rather than for some absolute level or near perfect goal. In this way, students compete against themselves.

Step 7: The teacher should praise improvements on the posting chart, using descriptive praise statements such as, "Billy, what a great job on your math assignment. You beat your best weekly score again!" It is also important to praise students who are having difficulty, but who are improving.

Step 8: Encourage peer comments and interaction about publicly posted information. If students compete against themselves rather than each other, spontaneous student comments will be positive.

Method 1: Acknowledge student's comments. For example, when a student makes a positive comment about a peer, the teacher might say, "Sarah, you are really sharp today. You noticed what a fantastic job Mary did on her math today."

Method 2: Provide additional information regarding student comments.

For example, if a student makes a positive comment about a peer, the teacher might say, "You're right, Bob. Tim not only finished **more** math problems today, but he beat his best score as well!"

Method 3: Praise students for making positive comments about other students.

Method 4: The teacher may enlist several popular students in the class to make positive comments about how others are doing. The teacher must stress to them that the comments must be sincere. With popular students making positive comments, others will soon follow suit.

In addition to these basic steps for implementing a public posting system, there are several advanced strategies that can improve the effects of a good public posting system even more. These strategies are described in How To Box 4-5.

Some teachers have expressed concern that students may feel uncomfortable if their work is displayed. Most students prefer a public posting system if it is used correctly and if positive information is displayed rather than negative. Public Posting, of course, should never be used to humiliate students. The more negative the system is, the less effective it will be. If teachers are concerned about posting student names, secret codes can be assigned instead.

Back-to-School Night is a good time for teachers to inform parents about the total classroom management plan, including the public posting system. The principal's support and permission should be obtained prior to presenting it to parents or students.

If it is designed correctly, the public posting system can boost the self-esteem of even slow learners (including Tough Kids). In fact, it has been shown that students in the bottom half of the class academically benefit from and improve most by the system.

Advanced Strategies for Public Posting

Advanced Strategy 1:

- Add a **tangible reward** for students who have improved their scores. In addition to the teacher's and peers' praise, the effect of public posting can be strengthened by adding Mystery Motivators, Spinners, or Grab-Bags. For example, the teacher can have all students who posted improvements for a particular day write their names on pieces of paper and put them in a container. The teacher then draws a name and gives the daily reward to the student whose name was drawn.

Advanced Strategy 2:

- To keep motivation high even when the teacher cannot immediately grade or evaluate the performance of all students, the teacher can randomly select several students at the end of the day and evaluate their performance. These students who have made improvements then have their work posted on a specially designed posted chart, and may be eligible for the reward described in Advanced Strategy 1.

Advanced Strategy 3:

- A classroom can be divided into teams with average team results posted. The team approach does not require that individual student names be posted, only a team name. However, both team and individual performance can be posted together, if desired.

Advanced Strategy 4:

- A very powerful way to use Public Posting is to combine it with a team-based group contingency. The classroom can be divided into teams as described in Advanced Strategy 3. Additionally, a reward is added for team performance. For example, each team may be given ten points each day. If a student breaks a rule or engages in misbehavior, one point is deducted from his/her team's total. The points that each team still maintains at the end of the day is publicly posted. Teams that are able to maintain a certain number of points over a week's time then win a treat or reward.

Contracts

When adults see the word "contract," they generally think of corporate mergers or sports stars signing agreements for millions of dollars. Contracts also have everyday meaning for most adults in terms of buying or renting cars, getting married, and business and employment agreements. Contracts are used in conjunction with many adult behaviors because they are explicit and set expectations. For similar reasons, contracts can also be used effectively when working with Tough Kids.

Following are a number of characteristics of contracts that must be present in order for them to be effective.

"Part 213, Section 1,079..."

- **Agreeing:** This means that both the teacher and the student have negotiated the consequences for specific behaviors. The negotiation aspect of a contract is one of its major advantages, particularly in working with adolescents who want to be adult-like and independent. Negotiations should not be one-sided in the sense that the teacher dictates terms to the student.

- **Formal Exchange:** The contracting equation is **Behavior = Reward**. It is always a mistake for teachers to relax the behavior requirement midway through a contract, to not give the agreed upon reward after the behavior has been produced, or to give the reward before the behavior is produced.

- **Reward or Penalty:** The positive consequence is the motivating component of a contract. However, it may also increase effectiveness to include a **penalty clause** if the agreed upon behavior is not produced within a certain time frame, or to offer a **bonus reward** if behavior is exceptional or produced before the specified deadline.

- **Behavior:** The expected behavior must be objectively defined (i.e., easily measured

or observed). It must include the **standard** that is expected (e.g., "B" grade or better) and the **time deadline** (e.g., by 3:00 P.M. next Friday).

Following are several approaches that will additionally enhance the effectiveness of contracting with Tough Kids.

- **Goal Setting:** Contracting can be combined with goal setting, with a student helping to set his/her own goals. If this procedure is used, a bonus reward for reaching the goal before the deadline and a penalty clause for not reaching the goal on time can be added.

- **Public Posting:** This procedure includes contracting for improvement and displaying the contract on a public bulletin board.

Group Contingencies: A contract can be designed for a total classroom or class teams instead of for an individual student. If this method is used, the teacher must be certain that each student in the group is capable of performing the expected behavior. An example of a group contingency might be for the teacher to formulate class teams that race each other on a United

States map from Los Angeles to New York. Each completed assignment contributes so many miles to the team (e.g., 100% = 100 miles; 75% = 75 miles). Speeding tickets can be given to teams for members' tardies or not turning in homework, which would deduct miles. Bonuses can be awarded on randomly selected days for the most mileage earned that day by a team.

- **Home Notes:** Contracts can be included in a Home Note program (see the Home Note section in this chapter). For example, when a student accumulates four weeks' worth of acceptable home notes, he/she receives an agreed upon reward or earns a Mystery Motivator.

The steps for implementing effective behavioral contracting are listed below:

Step 1: Define the specific behavior for which the contract is being implemented.

> **Poor examples** include: "improving classroom responsibility" or "showing respect for authority."

> **Better examples** include: "hand in work by the end of the period without being asked" or "talk in a calm voice to classmates with no arguing."

It may be necessary at first to break a behavior into smaller steps for the initial contract, so that the goal seems attainable to the student. It is important for the student to be successful initially in earning the contract reward so that he/she will be motivated to continue.

Step 2: Select contract reinforcers. The student should assist in this selection. Reinforcers should not take a lot of time to deliver, nor should they be expensive.

Step 3: Define the contract criteria. Generally, contract criteria include the quantity of behavior, quantity of reinforcer, and time limits. There are two basic types of contract criteria. These are **consecutive criteria** and **cumulative criteria**.

- Consecutive criteria are the least desirable type. For example, the student may be told that he/she will receive the contract reward if he/she earns 7 out of 10 recess points for ten straight days. In this case, the student may earn 7 points and above on nine days and earn 6 on the tenth, thus not receiving the reward.

- A better type of criteria is a cumulative criterion in which the quantity of behavior adds up with each student success but does not decrease for student failures. Cumulative criteria allow the student some days of not meeting the criteria.

Many contracts are defined so that they pay off at the end of the week. However, contracts can also be designed to pay off each day. Contracts that extend payoff over two weeks are generally poor, because a Tough Kid can seldom wait that long for payoff, at least initially. A rule of thumb for an initial contract is to pay off at least by the end of the week for a student with specified cumulative criteria.

Step 4: For a particularly unmotivated Tough Kid, consider adding a **bonus reward** and a **penalty clause**. A bonus reward is a helpful incentive for the student to reach his/her cumulative criteria quickly. While contracts should primarily be designed to be positive, the penalty clause may be added if the initial contract does not work even though the rewards are valued and the payoff time is short. An example of a penalty clause might be requiring the student to complete four homework assignments of "B" grade quality or better to receive the contract reward for the week (based on daily homework assignments for a five-day period). However, if the number of homework assignments is less than three for the week, the student loses television privileges at home for the next week. A penalty clause may be needed to give added incentive when all else fails.

Step 5: Negotiate the contract terms with the student. The basic substeps of negotiation are:

- Discuss a specific set of contract behaviors and rewards with the student.

- The teacher should indicate to the student why a contract is necessary and that he/she would like to help.

- Indicate that several of the contract components are negotiable (e.g., rewards, behaviors, criteria). Emphasize, however, that a contract is needed and its implementation is **not** negotiable.

- The teacher should tell the student what he/she would like to specify in the contract and ask for the student's input.

- Be careful not to allow the student to set unrealistically high standards for himself/herself. Encourage the student to begin slowly and then expand.

- The teacher should indicate that he/she wants and expects the contract to work, but that if things do not improve, a penalty clause will be added. Within limits, the penalty clause may be negotiated with the student.

- Tell the student that the contract is open to renegotiation at any time. The teacher should give the sense that he/she values the student's input.

Step 6: Put the terms of the contract in writing. Writing and signing a contract prevents misunderstandings and indicates agreement with the terms at the time that all parties sign the contract. Also, a good written contract will have a section that summarizes data on the student's progress (regardless of whether or not the contract criteria were met). By including these data, the contract will serve as a self-recording instrument. A written contract may also be publicly posted, further enhancing effectiveness.

Troubleshooting Contracts

No technique will work in all situations with Tough Kids. Although contracts can be powerful behavior change strategies when they are properly implemented, there can be problems with their use. Some common problems and their solutions are listed below.

Problem: The student starts out working hard and then loses motivation.

Solution: The reward payoff may be too delayed. Cut the time period before the reward can be earned in half. Delaying the reward too long is one of the most frequent problems with contracts.

Problem: The student appears confused and never really gets started.

Solution: The required behavior may not be defined or explained clearly enough, or too much of the required behavior may be expected initially. Discuss the expectations thoroughly with the student. If necessary, model and role play the behaviors. If the student understands, the requirement may be too great. Try reducing the behavior requirement for one week (half the problems, half the points, etc.). After at least one week when the student has received the contract reward, gradually begin to increase the contract requirement again.

Problem: The student still appears unmotivated and disinterested, even after the teacher has checked the delay in earning the reward, has checked for the student's understanding of the expectations, and the student has earned the contract reward at least once.

Solution: A penalty clause may be needed to get the student to actively participate.

Problem: The student began the contract excited about it, but appears frustrated and anxious before finishing.

Solution: Check the criteria. Student frustration can result from expectations that are too difficult. Use cumulative criteria rather than consecutive.

Problem: The student is openly defiant and will not participate in the contract.

Solution: The teacher should indicate to the student that he/she wants to negotiate the terms of the contract and values the student's input. If possible, invite an adult who is important to the student to participate in the negotiations, especially if a penalty clause is set. This person may be a parent, a coach, a favored teacher, a counselor, etc. Make certain the invited person supports the idea of a contract.

Problem: The parent(s) offer extremely large rewards with too long a time period before they are delivered (e.g., bicycle, four wheelers, trips, remote control vehicle, money).

Solution: The teacher should talk to the parent(s) and express his/her concern about the promised big reward. Help the parent(s) compile a list of smaller rewards to be given within a much shorter time period, and suggest the large reward as an additional bonus.

Cautions With Contracting

Teachers must remember that most contracts operate with a delayed reward payoff system. When working with Tough Kids, delays frequently destroy initial steps that are needed to get these students started. Contracts are most useful when: (1) They are used as a way of fading out more frequent rewards or after a student has started to perform appropriately, or (2) They are used with older or more motivated students. Contracts with long delays will be ineffective for younger or highly unmotivated students. In these cases, it is better to start with an hourly, twice daily, or daily reward system.

Parents and other professionals may object to a contract, believing that the student should just be responsible on his/her own. The problem is that the Tough Kid is **not** responsible. Thus, strategies are needed to get the student to begin to be responsible. Objectors may also see a contract as an artificial crutch. However, contracts should be designed to enhance initial motivation and eventually be slowly faded from use.

Some teachers may view contracts as too complex and time consuming. A well-designed contract is like a good investment. Most sound financial investments require initial start-up capital in order to return greater dividends later on. Similarly, a well-designed contract will take more time to implement than doing nothing. However, the potential dividends from implementing a contract are great.

Home Notes

The Home Note program is one of the most effective techniques for improving elementary and secondary students' motivation and classroom behavior. It is also one of the most mismanaged and underutilized techniques. The Home Note program consists simply of a note that (1) is periodically completed by the teacher; (2) is an assessment of academic and/or behavioral progress; (3) is sent home for the parent(s) to review, apply consequences to, and sign; and (4) is returned to school. How To Box 4-6 outlines the steps in setting up an effective Home Note program.

Problems can occur with even the best implemented Home Note program. The Home Note program is particularly prone to problems because it relies on a student to carry the note. However, most problems are readily resolvable if the program is well designed, and the teacher is working with cooperative parent(s).

"You don't have to read that Mom, just sign on the bottom."

Troubleshooting Home Notes

Problem: The student continues to lose the note.

Solution: Ask the parent(s) to take away a privilege at home or initiate a penalty when notes are not brought home. For example, the parent may have the student go to bed one hour early, or miss television or outside play time each day the note is not brought home. It is important that the teacher and parent(s) emphasize to the student that no excuses are accepted and that it is his/her responsibility to remember to ask the teacher for the note at the end of the school day and to bring it home.

Problem: The student changes the ratings or forges the teacher's initials.

Solution: Changing a rating or forging initials should be handled like a lost note. No excuses should be accepted, and the student should receive a penalty at home.

Problem: The student refuses to take the note home.

Solution: If the student flatly refuses to take the note, have the parent(s) consistently implement the procedures for a lost note. It will be important to be a support for the parent(s) in the event that this should occur. Most students will come around within a week, after having consequences applied consistently. The program may also be enhanced by providing reinforcement within the classroom for the student using the note properly, in addition to that provided by the parents.

How To Box 4-6

Implementing a Home Note Program

Step 1: Design or select a simple home note.

Step 2: Decide which behavior(s) will be targeted for change. Limit the selection to no more than five academic and/or social behaviors.

Step 3: Make contact with the student's parent(s) either in person or by phone to gain their cooperation and explain the system. With parental input, determine what positive or mild negative consequences the parents are willing to deliver at home depending on the student's home note performance.

Ask the parent(s) to read the note each day, make certain it is initialed by the teacher, and sign it to indicate that they have read the note. Convince the parents to accept **no** excuses for the student not bringing the note home.

Step 4: Decide when the Home Note program will start and how frequently home notes will be given. It is generally more effective to begin by giving the home note each day and slowly fade to giving the note only on Fridays, and finally fade to no note.

Step 5: Explain the program to the student, and answer any questions the student has about the program.

Step 6: Implement the program. After marking the note, give the student specific feedback as to what he/she did right, and what needs to improve. Encourage the student!

Step 7: Once the program has been implemented, call the parent(s) at least twice the first week and once a week for the next two weeks afterwards to troubleshoot problems and provide support to the parent(s) for their part in the program.

Step 8: After the program has been in place for four to six weeks, arrange for another parent conference or talk with the parent(s) by phone to review the student's progress. Be sure to be optimistic and emphasize the gains the student has made. The teacher should discuss any concerns he/she or the parent(s) have with the program, make any needed adjustments, and plan to continue the program as needed.

Problem: The parents are willing to look at the note, but they are incapable of applying consequences at home for the program.

Solution: Put together a reinforcer kit which is delivered to the home (e.g., candy, stickers, little toys) that the parent(s) can give the student for a good note.

An alternative is for the teacher to tell the parent(s) that he/she would like to begin applying the consequences for the note in the classroom. The parent(s) are still expected to review and sign the note at home. When it is returned the next day, class reinforcers such as a Mystery Motivator, Spinner, or a Grab-Bag may be given or a mild negative consequence such as missing recess, staying after school, or eating lunch in the classroom may be delivered.

Problem: The teacher suspects that the parent(s) may be abusive to the student if he/she receives a poor note.

Solution: Set up a meeting with the parent(s) and ask for their cooperation in applying **agreed** upon consequences (both positive and negative). Tell them that if they punish too severely the program will fail, and the student will learn to dislike school. If abuse continues, the program may have to be discontinued or authorities called. Although this is a serious problem when it occurs, it rarely comes up.

Problem: Parent(s) refuse to participate in the program and will not even sign the note.

Solution: Set up a meeting with the parent(s). Address any concerns they have with the program. Explain that the program is not designed to punish the student, but to give the student feedback about his/her performance and to keep the parent(s) informed. Ask if they would be willing to try the program for two weeks. If they still refuse, the teacher should tell them that he/she would like to give the student the note anyway, and hopes they will look at it. (In this case, try to make the notes as positive as possible for the first week.)

Beeper Tapes

Tough Kids exhibit many behaviors that interfere with their learning and interpersonal relationships in the classroom. Given independent assignments to complete in their seats, Tough Kids may talk to their classmates, leave their seats, disrupt the class, or worse. During group instruction they may not watch or listen while the teacher presents a critical new skill, avoid responding when called on to do so, and may disturb students around them so that they cannot profit from the instruction either. A "beeper tape" program provides a means to improve classroom behavior of these students.

The use of beeper tapes systematically provides positive reinforcement for increasing amounts of appropriate behavior. Once appropriate behavior has been established and stabilized at acceptable levels, the use of the beeper tapes is gradually withdrawn. Fading the tapes is necessary to avoid students' dependence on the tapes and to enable them to function successfully with less supervision and in other school settings.

What are Beeper Tapes?

Tough Kid beeper tapes are a series of 30- or 45-minute audio cassette tapes on which an unpredictable series of audible "beeps" have been recorded. When one of the tapes is being played on a tape player in the classroom, targeted individual students (or the entire class) earn a point or token (such as poker chips, marbles, or class "money") each time a beep sounds and they are doing what they are supposed to be doing.

Beeper tapes are designed so that some of the Tough Kid's appropriate behavior, but not all of it, will result in positive reinforcement. This is referred to as **intermittent reinforcement**. Behaviors that are positively reinforced on an intermittent basis are more likely to be maintained over the long run. When intermittent reinforce-

ment is used correctly, the student learns to delay gratification and maintain appropriate behavior over longer and longer periods of time.

Pointer Box 4-3 lists sources for teachers to obtain beeper tapes.

Steps for Using Beeper Tapes

1. Explain to target students (or the class) the exact behaviors they are expected to exhibit in order to earn a point or token when the "beep" sounds. Then explain how the beeper tape program works.

2. Select the beeper tape with the appropriate number of beeps. In selecting a beeper tape,

---

Pointer Box 4-3

Obtaining Beeper Tapes

Teachers can make their own sets of beeper tapes by using an audio cassette recorder, a clock with a second hand, and a device with which to make a noise. Teachers have used such simple things as a doorbell or hitting an empty glass with a spoon to make the noise. The teacher can make a full set of six tapes or only the tapes currently needed according to the specifications below. For 30-minute tapes, the following schedule for a full set of six tapes is relevant:

20 beeps = average of 1 beep every	1 1/2 minutes
15 beeps = average of 1 beep every	2 minutes
10 beeps = average of 1 beep every	3 minutes
5 beeps = average of 1 beep every	6 minutes
3 beeps = average of 1 beep every	10 minutes
2 beeps = average of 1 beep every	15 minutes

The *Practice Skills Mastery Program* is a published teacher's manual that includes a graduated set of six beeper tapes. The manual gives specific step-by-step instructions on how to implement a beeper tape program in the classroom. The program is available for a cost of $45.00 at the following address:

Mastery Programs, Ltd.
P.O. Box 90
Logan, Utah 84321

the teacher will begin with the tape on which the average length of time between beeps approximates or is slightly greater than the amount of time the target student follows classroom rules before engaging in inappropriate behavior.

Example:

Mary Beth currently breaks classroom rules on the average of six times during the 30-minute reading session. This amounts to one rule infraction every five minutes. Mr. Johnson selects the tape with five beeps per 30 minutes (an average of one beep every six minutes), since this schedule approximates the time frame of misbehavior that Mary Beth currently exhibits.

3. Select a method for recording points or tokens that students (or the class) earn.

    - This may be an **individual point card** taped to students' desks or carried by students. The teacher can mark the cards or have students mark their own when asked.

    - A **group point sheet** may be carried on a clipboard by the teacher and marked as points are earned. Each time a beep sounds, the teacher must tell students if they have earned a point. At the end of the academic period the teacher transfers points earned onto students' individual cards.

    Variations:

    - Trade points earned for Chart Moves.

    - Have the class earn points collectively toward a class reward.

4. Decide what points or tokens may be traded for. (A Spinner may be appropriately used for payoffs.) Initially rewards should be earned daily if students are earning 85% of their points or better.

5. When a beep sounds, the teacher should give immediate and specific verbal praise to target students (or the class) who are doing what they are supposed to be doing and inform them that they have earned a point or token. (**NOTE:** The old adage to "let sleeping dogs lie" is never appropriate when using beeper tapes. The beep sound is the teacher's cue to immediately praise deserving students.)

Examples:

"John, Steve and Gina, you've just earned a point for working on your math sheets. Great job!"

"Ashley, I appreciate your watching me and listening. That's a point for you."

"Wow, the whole class was practicing their reading paragraph just now! Everyone earned a point."

6. As appropriate behavior increases, the teacher should use beeper tapes with longer intervals and fewer beeps. When should the teacher move to the next tape? Whether the teacher is using the beeper tapes for only one or two students or for the entire class, he/she will begin using the next tape in the series when the payoff criteria of 85% of possible points has been earned for three consecutive days.

    Any time the teacher begins using a new tape and the students are not meeting criteria within the first three days, the teacher should drop back to the previous tape at which the students were successful. If dropping back is necessary, the teacher should again require three days of meeting criteria before beginning to use the next tape again.

Beeper tape payoffs will automatically become less frequent as longer intervals are introduced and there are fewer beeps on the tape. In this way, positive reinforcement will gradually be reduced.

Box 4-2

Cautions for Using Beeper Tapes

- For some students the teacher will need to adjust the number of points required for payoffs as longer intervals of appropriate behavior are demonstrated. In other words, if a student demonstrates appropriate behavior for longer intervals but still needs daily payoffs to meet criteria, the teacher will need to continue to provide daily payoffs for the time being.

- The teacher should **never** discontinue using specific praise statements for appropriate behavior, even when the beeps have been reduced or eliminated.

Box 4-2 offers two cautions for teachers using the beeper tape program.

It is assumed that if teacher praise alone were positively reinforcing enough to Tough Kids to begin with, the teacher could simply praise them for their appropriate behavior in order to increase it. If this were the case, beeper tapes would not be needed. For many Tough Kids, however, teacher praise simply is not powerful enough initially to be effective. Rather, these students must **actually be taught** to find it reinforcing. Thus, with the beeper tape program, **praise must be paired with the giving of points or tokens** which are then exchangeable for items or activities the students already find to be positively reinforcing. Gradually, as beeps (and thus points) are reduced and then withdrawn, teacher praise will retain the positive reinforcement qualities students have learned to associate with it. Teacher praise, then, must never be completely eliminated, since it is the praise that will continue to maintain students' newly improved behavior. Teachers must let Tough Kids know what it is that they are doing right and that they appreciate it.

How To Box 4-7 offers some suggestions for troubleshooting beeper tape programs.

Weaning Tough Kids From Beeper Tapes

When Tough Kids can successfully work and/or follow classroom rules for at least 15 consecutive minutes, the teacher may begin moving toward a less cumbersome means of increasing appropriate classroom behavior:

1. Without the use of beeper tapes, the teacher will award points earned at the end of productive 15-minute work periods (e.g., if a maximum of five points can be earned, the

How To Box 4-7

Trouble-shooting Beeper Tape Programs

If students are not meeting beeper tape criteria after three days with a particular tape, consider the following suggestions:

- Examine classroom expectations. Do students know exactly what the teacher wants them to do?

- Change or adjust the positive reinforcement that students can earn for meeting criteria.

- Lower the number of points needed for payoff.

Eliminate students from the group (classroom) payoffs if they are deliberately sabotaging group efforts. Keep the rest of the class on the same payoff schedule, but place the single student on an individual payoff schedule.

- Drop back to a tape with smaller intervals between beeps.

teacher might award four points if the student talked out or broke another rule). The teacher will gradually increase work periods to 20 minutes, 30 minutes, one hour, etc.

2. When students are working successfully for 15 minutes with the system described above, the teacher may have the students begin to monitor and evaluate their own work and behavior. In this way, responsibility will gradually be shifted from teacher to students. (See the Self-Management section of this chapter for further details.)

Peer Tutoring

There are a number of benefits for both Tough Kids and their peers from a good peer tutoring program in the classroom. Academic gains, improvement in classroom behavior, and cooperative peer relations have been common positive outcomes of peer tutoring programs. Teachers should note, however, that peer tutoring techniques are most effective when they are used to **supplement** teacher instruction rather than to take its place. To maximize effectiveness, Tough Kids and their tutors must be carefully taught the specific procedures to be used, and the teacher must monitor the program carefully.

"So, do you get it?"

Class-wide peer tutoring programs are relatively easy to implement. How To Box 4-8 provides step-by-step instructions for implementation.

An initial time investment by the teacher to thoroughly train students in their roles will pay big dividends in the long run. Each step must be carefully explained to students, and they must have the opportunity to ask questions and gain clarification. Supervised role playing with corrective feedback from the teacher as well as discussion may be helpful. Specific error correction procedures and the use of tokens or points must be carefully reviewed and demonstrated.

How To Box 4-8

Implementing a
Peer Tutoring Program

- The teacher will decide on a subject for tutoring, and select a 30-minute period of the day for the program. (Within the 30 minutes allotted, the peer will tutor the Tough Kid for ten minutes, the Tough Kid will tutor the peer for ten minutes, and ten minutes will be spent by both counting points and posting results.

- Tough Kid and peer pairs will be selected and reassigned once each week. They will sit next to or across from each other during tutoring sessions. The teacher will tell each pair who will tutor first. The tutor will monitor performance (e.g., oral reading), correct errors, and award points for correct performance. The teacher signals at the end of ten minutes that roles are to reverse.

- The teacher circulates among the pairs of students during peer tutoring sessions and awards points for tutoring correctly. He/she may also divide the class into two teams (e.g., rows one and two competing with rows three and four).

- When both ten-minute tutoring sessions are over, both the Tough Kid and the peer each count their own and the other's points. When the teacher calls on the pair, they will verbally report points earned. The teacher will publicly post the scores at the front of the room on the blackboard or on a poster. Points are tallied, and the winning pair and/or team is announced. Each week the composition of the pairs or teams changes. Small rewards may be given both on a daily basis (as needed) as well as on a weekly basis.

- At least once each week, the teacher will conduct his/her own evaluation of each students' progress on skills practiced with peer tutoring teams.

Sources: Delquadri, Greenwood, Stretton, & Hall (1983); Greenwood, Delquadri, & Hall (1984).

Self-Management

Self-management techniques have been used successfully with Tough Kids to increase their appropriate behaviors, such as improving academic skills and performance of on-task behavior. They have also been very effective in decreasing Tough Kids' inappropriate behaviors.

The ultimate goal of self-management procedures is the management or control by Tough Kids of their own behavior—a goal most educators wholeheartedly support! While Tough Kids may manage their own behavior in the long run after using these techniques, usually the teacher will need to be the primary manager initially. However, the teacher's objective will be to gradually transfer as much management of the Tough Kids' behavior from the teacher to the students themselves as is possible during the course of the intervention.

One advantage of teaching Tough Kids to evaluate and monitor their own behavior, of course, is that they then need to depend less on the teacher for guidance, reinforcement, and control. Emphasis on this self-management approach is relevant to teacher concerns regarding time demands placed on them by interventions which rely solely on their own efforts. Tough Kids who learn to self-manage are not only active participants in their own improved performance, but they perceive themselves as more competent as well. Additionally, self-management skills are "portable" in that they rely mainly on the students themselves for implementation. Thus, there is a great deal of appeal for teachers in teaching self-management skills to Tough Kids. How To Box 4-9 details the necessary steps to teach Tough Kids to self-manage their own behavior.

Some self-management techniques are very simple to use. For example, Tough Kids may be given a piece of paper with 20 or so squares marked on it. Students can be taught to make a plus sign (+) in one of the squares each time they "think about" and "recognize" that they are working or behaving appropriately. A minus (-) sign is to be used when they think they are not working or behaving appropriately. Pluses can be converted to points which can be exchanged for rewards.

With very young children, a "smiley face" may be used to denote very appropriate behavior or working, while a "frowny face" indicates poor working or behavior. A "neutral face" indicates OK or fair behavior or working.

One way teachers can enhance the use of self-management procedures is through the use of a "matching" procedure. Once a teacher has transferred at least some of the responsibility for rating and marking down the student's behavior to the student, the teacher may continue to rate and mark the behavior **some of the time**. If this is done on a random basis, the student will not know ahead of time when the teacher ratings will take place. When the teacher "matches"

How To Box 4-9

Implementing a Self-Management Program

1. **Begin to introduce self-management soon after the behavior has reached an acceptable level with the teacher managing it.**

2. **Specifically define the behavior the student will monitor and evaluate.** The teacher must explain exactly what behavior is to be monitored and exactly how it will be recorded. Giving examples and nonexamples of the behavior and role playing can be very helpful.

3. **Design a simple means of counting and recording the behavior.** The simpler the system the more accurate the student is likely to be in counting and recording the behavior.

4. **Set time limits.** Predetermine periods of 15, 30, or 60 minutes during which the student will count and record behavior. Most students will find monitoring their behavior indefinitely too overwhelming. The teacher may wish to begin with a small period of time and gradually increase to a longer time period as the student becomes more proficient.

5. **Check the student's accuracy on a random basis.** Rewards should be built-in for students who are counting and recording their behavior accurately.

6. **Give the student ample opportunity to practice the process of self-management and provide positive, corrective feedback.**

ratings with a student, a bonus point is given for exact matches, the student keeps his/her own ratings when there are only one to two points difference between teacher and student ratings, and the student loses all points for that rating period when there is a bigger difference than one to two points between the teacher and student ratings.

Self-management skills are not a panacea. However, there is good evidence that they can be very helpful in working with Tough Kids if they receive very specific instruction on how to use the program, control of how the students behave and work is **gradually** moved from the teacher to the students, and the teacher continues to carefully monitor students' correct and accurate use of the program.

Parent Training

Working with the parents of Tough Kids may be the only way a teacher can affect change in the student's home. However, many teachers simply give up on working with parents because they believe it is too difficult. Most parenting programs actually lose about 50% of parents after they are begun. But why? It may not be because the parents are too difficult to work with. It may be that educators train them incorrectly and/or with the wrong materials.

There are several common mistakes made by teachers that result in parents not coming to training sessions. The biggest mistake is to make the parents of Tough Kids feel that they are the cause of the problem. Most parents of Tough Kids have had years of negative contact with school personnel who insinuate that their family lives are at the root of the students' problems. Parents must be made to feel comfortable and part of a team effort at the first meeting.

The second basic problem with parent training is that many parenting programs focus on mild issues and problems. But parents of Tough Kids are plagued by the same problems at home as their children's teachers are at school. Good programs for parents of Tough Kids focus on changing arguing, aggression, noncompliance, tantrums, poor school performance, and problems with social skills.

Third, many parenting programs are far too technical and complex. Professional jargon,

theoretical concepts, and difficult data collection requirements result in parents dropping out. Parents should be made to feel comfortable, competent, and helped to see the immediate connection with what is suggested in training and meaningful behavior change.

There are several "tricks of the trade" that make parent traning effective. First, the teacher should disclose a little about himself/herself. If he/she has children, the teacher should talk about them in human terms. The teacher should talk about personal difficulties and how he/she applies the techniques that are being suggested to other parents. If the teacher does not have children, he/she should talk about using the suggested solutions in the classroom. The teacher must present himself/herself as not perfect, but working to manage problems.

Second, the teacher should be humorous. Getting parents to laugh breaks down barriers and makes the whole training session enjoyable. Third, if possible, the parents should be trained in a group (although individual training can be effective). Working with parents in a group maximizes the teacher's efforts and helps parents see that other parents have similar problems with their children. During the first training meeting, parents should describe their child (age and sex), what they like about them, and what they would like to change.

Fourth, the teacher should use a structured curriculum or set of materials that focuses on meaningful behaviors (arguing, noncomplinace, aggression, academic problems, etc.). It helps if there is a book for the parents to use as a guide. Pointer Box 4-4 lists several good parenting programs and parent resource books.

Fifth, the teacher should use as many prompts and techniques as possible to keep parents interested. For examples, video tapes and films (audio tapes are not recommended), overheads, cartoons to illustrate points, or role playing all help. Sixth, the teacher should give parents homework assignments after each meeting so they build a system of behavior change.

If the teacher finds he/she is losing parents, particularly low income parents, it may help to: (1) call before each parent group, (2) supply baby-sitting (volunteers), or (3) supply some type of transportation or a gasoline coupon (donation from a gasoline company or a bus pass).

A sample weekly training sequence is listed in How To Box 4-10. This sample sequence closely parallels the procedures presented in this book. With slight modification, the techniques can be used by parents at home. This sequence focuses on recruiting parents as part of the school-home team. The first night of training is spent on having parents describe their children and learning what causes childhood problems. The goal is to make parents feel comfortable and

Pointer Box 4-4

Suggested Parent Training Materials

Families
    G. Patterson
    Research Press
    2612 North Mattis Avenue
    Champaign, IL 61821

Parents and Adolescents Living Together
    (*Parts 1 & 2*)
    G. Patterson & M. Forgatch
    Castalia Publishing
    P.O. Box 1587
    Eugene, OR 97440

Parents and Children Series
    C. Webster-Stratton
    Castalia Publishing
    P.O. Box 1587
    Eugene, OR 97440

Parents On Your Side and *Assertive Discipline for Parents*
    L. Canter & M. Canter
    Lee Canter and Associates
    P.O. Box 2112
    Santa Monica, CA 90407-2113

Parent Training for Tough Kids
    W.R. Jenson
    Preferred Practices Press
    1171 First Avenue
    Salt Lake City, UT 84103

Solving Child Behavior Problems at Home and School
    E. Blechman
    Research Press
    2612 North Mattis Avenue
    Champaign, IL 61821

SOS: Help for Parents
    L. Clark
    Parents' Press
    P.O. Box 2180
    Bowling Green, KY 42102-2180

Troubled Families: A Treatment Program
    M. Fleischman, A. Horne, & J. Arthur
    Research Press
    2612 North Mattis Avenue
    Champaign, IL 61821

How To Box 4-10

Parenting Tough Kids Training–Sample Sequence

Week 1: Introduction—Making Parents Part of the Team

- Setting the tone (humor, self-disclosure, and practical target behaviors)
- Parents describe their child (what they like, what they want to change)
- Temperament and its effects on behavior
- Parent homework: Select three behaviors to increase and select reinforcers to use

Week 2: Increasing Positive and Differential Attention

- Homework review
- IFEED-AV reinforcement rules
- Differential attention
- Parent homework: using differential attention

Week 3: Decreasing Noncompliance

- Homework review
- The coercive process explained
- Using antecedents (effective request making) to reduce noncompliance—precision requests
- Using reductive consequences to stop noncompliance–time out
- Parent homework: Giving precision requests followed by reductive consequences for noncompliance

Week 4: The "Sure I Will" Program and Noncompliance in Public Settings

- Homework review
- Reducing noncompliance in public settings
- The "Sure I Will" program
- Unique motivators (Mystery Motivators, Spinners, Grab-Bags)
- Parent homework: Setting up a "Sure I Will" program

Week 5: The Home-to-School Connection

- Homework review
- The Home Note program
- Learning to design a behavioral contract
- Parent homework: Setting up a Home Note program

Week 6: Social Skills, Homework, and Parent Tutoring

- Homework review
- Learning about social skills curricula
- Learning to set up an effective homework program
- Learning to set up an effective parent tutoring program
- Finishing the group

Adapted from Jenson (1984).

not accuse them of causing students' difficulties.

During the second meeting, improving the overall positive interactions with the children and teaching differential attention as an alternative to reprimanding is stressed. During the third meeting, coercion and how to reduce children's "pain control" through effective antecedents (precision requests) and practical reductive consequences are explained. The time out technique for use at home is introduced.

During the fourth meeting, the use of precision requests in public places is explained, and the "Sure I Will" program, a method for positively reinforcing compliance, is introduced. The use of Mystery Motivators, reinforcement Spinners, and Grab-Bags as rewards is explained.

During the fifth meeting, the home-to-school connection is introduced with the Home Note program. Parents are taught to design and begin the Home Note program as a method of communicating with the teacher and helping manage their Tough Kids' behavior in the classroom.

During the sixth meeting, advanced techniques, which include an overview of social skills curricula that can be used at home and setting up an effective homework or parent tutoring program are offered.

There are several effective parent training programs that can be used with the parents of Tough Kids. The important goal is to recruit the parents as part of a coordinated team that works between the students' homes and the classroom. The closer the parent training interventions parallel what the teacher does in the classroom, the better the overall result for students. Parents are valuable resources that teachers should incorporate.

Summary

The critical information necessary to design and implement effective programs for teachers' toughest students has now been covered. Once effective interventions have been selected from this book and implemented, what can and should be done to keep things working? One of the most common errors that teachers of Tough Kids make is to set up interventions and then assume that they will continue to be effective almost indefinitely. The key to managing Tough Kids effectively is to view planning for their program as an **ongoing process** which will require regular attention.

After initial implementation, there are bound to be problem areas which do not continue to work as well as they should. The teacher will want to review relevant parts of this book to identify problem areas early on, analyze them, make adjustments to the Tough Kid's program, continue implementation, continue to analyze, and so on. Only by engaging in ongoing evaluation and adjustments based on that evaluation will the program continue to meet the Tough Kid's needs.

References

Carnine, D. & Silbert, J. (1979). *Direct instruction reading*. Columbus, OH: Merrill Publishing.

Delquadri, J.D., Greenwood, C.R., Stretton, K., & Hall, R.V. (1983). The peer tutoring spelling game: A classroom procedure for increasing opportunity to respond and spelling performance. *Education and Treatment of Children, 6,* 225-239.

Greenwood, C.R., Delquadri, J.D., & Hall, R.V. (1984). Opportunity to respond and student academic performance. In W.L. Heward, T.E. Heron, D.S. Hill, & J. Trap-Porter (Eds.), *Focus on behavior analysis in education*. Columbus, OH: Merrill Publishing.

Jenson, W.R. (1984). *Parent training for tough kids*. Salt Lake City, UT: Preferred Practices Press.

Johnson, D.W. & Johnson, R.T. (1980). Integrating handicapped students into the mainstream. *Exceptional Children, 47,* 90-98.

Johnson, D.W. & Johnson, R.T. (1986). Mainstreaming and cooperative learning strategies. *Exceptional Children, 52,* 553-561.

Morgan, D.P. & Jenson, W.R. (1988). *Teaching behaviorally disordered students: Preferred practices*. Columbus, OH: Merrill Publishing.